S[illegible] by People [illegible] ifficulties

by
Andrea Whittaker
Simon Gardner
Joyce Kershaw

based on

The People First Report

An Evaluation of Services in
London Borough of Hillingdon
March, 1990

Published by the King's Fund Centre
126 Albert Street
London
NW1 7NF

Tel: 071 267 6111

ISBN 1 85717 002 4

Distributed by Bailey Distribution Ltd
Dept KFP
Learoyd Road
Mountfield Industrial Estate
New Romney
Kent
TN28 8XU

The King's Fund Centre is a health services development agency which promotes improvements in health and social care. We do this by working with people in health services, in social services, in voluntary agencies, and with the users of their services. We encourage people to try out new ideas, provide financial or practical support to new developments, and enable experiences to be shared through workshops, conferences and publications. Our aim is to ensure that good developments in health and social care are widely taken up.

The King's Fund Centre is a part of the
King Edward's Hospital Fund for London.

Thank you to:

The people who live in the houses who allowed us into their lives and welcomed us so warmly whenever we arrived. We feel we made new friends.

The staff in the houses who did so much to make our job easier. We could not have done the work without their willing co-operation.

Philip Brownbill and Gill McLean of Hillingdon Social Services for 'smoothing the path' for us in a variety of ways.

Roger Blunden, Ken Simons, Liz Winn and Lynne Woodward for valuable advice during the compiling of this publication and to Maureen Eldridge and Melanie Kornitzer for patiently producing numerous drafts.

All the People First members and supporters who advised and helped, including:

Tony Balster
Peter Broadbridge
Michael Brookstein
Gary Bourlet
Sue Charles
Bruce Charles
Alice Etherington
Denise Grayston
John Sims
Christine Vandervord
Cathy Walls
Judith Wood
Janet Wright

Foreword

This evaluation looked at just one corner of one authority's services for people with learning difficulties. North West Thames Regional Health Authority funded People First to do this evaluation in order to ask people's views about what services they were getting, what they wanted, what was important to them. That will be possible only if people have or are given the opportunity to say what they want and what they think about the services they are getting, or indeed not getting.

The report may appear to be complicated. The evaluation was really very simple. So why cannot we adopt this approach universally? It just needs a bit of courage to be prepared to listen to the real experts, people who experience our services every day.

Service users do not feel free to comment honestly to the staff who provide the services. The users are dependent on the service and may fear what will happen to them if they are too outspoken. However, People First consultants, as service users themselves, were able to report frankly to service managers. As consultants and speakers on a platform when they reported their work, People First earned respect for themselves and for the people whose services they were investigating.

What I hope this report does is to stimulate you into devising your own ways of putting service users at the heart of service design and evaluation. We did it one way in Hillingdon, there will be many other ways which service users themselves will discover as they gain expertise in evaluation.

I can commend Hillingdon to you as the place where the health and local authorities pooled all their resources for people with learning difficulties, years in advance of Caring for People. I can also commend North West Thames as a Region which is trying to get to grips with giving power to service users. Last year we resettled 238 people from hospital into normal, ordinary lifestyles and we need to work hard to learn from those people.

David Pashley
Director
Community Care Office
North West Thames Regional Health Authority

Contents

Introduction

Consumerism, user-friendly services, the voice of the patient – all these are currently 'buzz words' in health and social services. Government documents emphasise the importance of the user's voice and many of the organisational changes now taking place in services, are said to enable service users to be partners with professionals in achieving better lives for people.

With regard to people with learning difficulties, it is now generally accepted that they should have a voice in how services are planned and delivered. They have a right to be involved in influencing the direction that services are taking.

So, how far have we got in turning the good words into action? It is fair to say we have become better at listening to what people want. We have worked out better ways of consulting people. Many People First members, for example, have taken part in consultation exercises which made sure that people with learning difficulties could be effectively involved. But when we go beyond consultation to active participation, good examples are much more difficult to find.

This publication records one such example. It has been produced not only to present the results of this evaluation, but to encourage other people and organisations to give service users similar opportunities. It is written to be used by both professionals and service users.

Background

North West Thames Regional Health Authority wanted a service users' view of the lives of people with learning difficulties now moving from institutions into ordinary houses in the community as part of its hospital closure programme. The Region asked for a down-to-earth look at services from the point of view of a person using the service – what is happening in people's lives now – how do they feel about their lives – what do they want in the future. On this occasion, a sophisticated, research-based evaluation full of charts and figures was not expected: the sort of evaluation which, as one person stated, often 'really tells you nothing!'.

People First was invited to do this work because of its experience as an organisation run by and for people with learning difficulties. People First began in the United States and has been established in the UK for the past six years. It has become a national focus for encouraging and developing self-advocacy around the country. Its members have gained considerable skills in speaking up for themselves and advocating on behalf of people with learning difficulties generally.

With regard to this evaluation, People First had the advantage of being an independent organisation and so could give an independent opinion of services. Also, its members know from personal experience what they are talking about – they can relate to people with learning difficulties in a way which is not possible for either staff or professional researchers.

Hillingdon Social Services was a very appropriate third partner in the initiative as the borough had already demonstrated its commitment to including service users in the planning and development of services.

It believes very firmly in 'listening to people carefully' and building services around what people want. It has developed practical ways of achieving this. Senior staff make time to be out and about talking to people face-to-face, both as individuals and in groups. Service users are involved as members of special consultation groups, such as the August Group, where service users join with staff in considering the needs of people with disabilities in Hillingdon.

The borough has actively encouraged self-advocacy by providing opportunities, backed up with resources, for people with learning difficulties to speak up for themselves and say what they want from services. It was one of the first boroughs to provide funds for a People First group to meet in an ordinary venue in the community – a small but important step in helping the group become more independent of services.[1]

How People First became involved

People First was first contacted in July 1989 about the possibility of doing the evaluation. The proposal was put to a People First meeting in October of that year and agreed. It was felt that this was an exciting opportunity to be involved in a very important part of the development of services. It was an important recognition of the value of the opinion of people who use the services. It could be used as an example for people in other parts of the country and encourage them to do the same thing.

Why this evaluation is unique

Much valuable work has already been done by researchers both here and abroad on how to make the views of service users an integral part of creating quality services. They have explored various ways of obtaining service users' views and have evaluated the effectiveness of different methods. This work is well documented, and in the last section of this book we give suggestions for further reading.

We know of a few instances where individual groups of people with learning difficulties have devised their own questionnaires in order to find out more about the lives of people in their local hospital, hostel or day centre and we found one recorded example of this, involving students at a day centre in Derbyshire.[2]

However, as far as we are aware, this is the first time that people with learning difficulties have been given the task – with the necessary back-up resources – of undertaking an evaluation of services to their peer group. People with learning difficulties themselves drew up the questionnaires, carried out the interviews and agreed the conclusions. This evaluation put service users 'in the driving seat' – calling on support and skills from other people as needed.

Brief description of the evaluation

For a detailed account of what the evaluation involved, how it was done and what it revealed about the lives of the people living in Hillingdon, readers should turn to Part I of this publication. Here we give a very brief summary to 'set the scene'.

Preparation for the evaluation began in February 1990 with a consultation meeting of People First members who all had experience of living in institutions and in the community. Information collected at this meeting formed the base from which the questionnaires were developed.

Two members of People First, Simon Gardner and Joyce Kershaw, were the consultants who carried out the evaluation. They were supported by Andrea Whittaker, a Senior Project Officer in the Community Living Development Team at the King's Fund Centre. The consultants and their supporter spent two weeks in

March 1990 looking at the lives of seven people living in two houses in the London Borough of Hillingdon. Information was collected using formal interviews, informal interviews and observation. The report was handed to North West Thames RHA in July, 1990.

The evaluation was itself evaluated by Libby Cooper, Director of Charities Evaluation Services. A copy of Libby's report can be found in Part II of this publication.

PART I

THE PEOPLE FIRST REPORT

An evaluation of services in London Borough of Hillingdon March, 1990

1 Setting the Scene*

Hillingdon chose two houses to be the subject of this evaluation. In one house the three people had been living there for nine months at the time of the evaluation. In the second house, the four people had been living there for four months. Some doubts were expressed about choosing these two houses; were they too new to be evaluated? Would it not be better to choose places which had been operating for a longer time? However, the funding for the evaluation was coming from the hospital closure programme, and these houses were part of that programme. People First would be giving their opinion of what they saw in the houses at a particular point in time, which could provide a baseline for later comparisons. As for the people living in the houses, comparisons between their former life and their present life would be fresh in their minds.

Valley Road

This is a compact, two-storey, end-of-terrace house, situated in the far corner of a large housing estate on the south side of the borough. It is 10–15 minutes walk to the main road and the nearest bus stop, and 25 minutes walk to the nearest station. There is a small, local shop on the estate about 5 minutes walk from the house. Three people live there with support from staff who come in several times during the week.

Prince Street

This is a spacious, 1930s-style bungalow situated at the end of a short residential close on the north side of the borough. It is a 5 minute walk through a back lane to the bus-stop, a pub and a small group of local shops. Four men live there, supported by staff on a 24-hour basis.

* The names of the residents and all places associated with them have been changed.

2 The Evaluation Team

The Consultants

Joyce Kershaw
Joyce is a member of People First and has been a leader in the People First group in Huddersfield since it began in 1986. She is skilled at speaking up for herself and on behalf of other people, and has developed considerable expertise in negotiating for changes in people's lives.

Simon Gardner
Simon is a member of People First and has been active in the London and Thames group for several years. He has considerable experience of speaking at conferences and taking part in training workshops.

More details of Joyce and Simon's life and work experiences are given in the appendices.

The Supporter

Andrea Whittaker
Andrea is a Senior Project Officer in the Community Living Development Team at the King's Fund Centre and has been working in services to people with learning difficulties for the past twenty years. For the last six years, she has been particularly involved with self advocacy through helping to get People First established. She was Adviser to the organisation until it set up its own office in October, 1989.

Andrea provided support at all stages of developing the questionnaires and helped with recording the information. Her role also included making the administrative arrangements, organising the timetable and providing the transport and accommodation.

Someone to 'evaluate' us

We felt it was important to have an independent person with experience of doing evaluations to comment on our work. We felt this was particularly important because this type of evaluation has not been attempted before. We were fortunate that *Libby Cooper*, then Director of CRAC (Community Research Advisory Centre) was able to take on this role.

It was agreed that Libby's contribution would be twofold:

(a) an observational role – but intervening if she felt there was anything vital to mention; and

(b) evaluating the project with the 'objective eye' of the professional researcher, and providing a brief report on her findings.

We had two meetings with Libby, during which we discussed such matters as: maintaining objectivity; the need to compare people's lives now with what they were like before; the possibility that residents may find it difficult to be critical; areas which should be included in the evaluation; practical details about how to record information.

3 Method

Summary of key dates

17 January	Lunch at Hillingdon with various members of staff and two people from the houses, followed by a meeting with link person at Hillingdon to discuss details of the work.
13 February	Consultation with members of People First.
20 February	Meeting with the independent evaluator.
28 February	'Package' agreed with N.W. Thames RHA.
27 February–14 March	Preparation/developing questionnaires.
16 March	First meeting at Prince Street.
17 March	First meeting at Valley Road.
19–31 March	Two weeks: evaluation.
3 & 5 April	Remaining two interviews and starting to look at results.
9 May	Presentation of preliminary results at Hillingdon.

Consulting People First members

The evaluation process began with a consultation meeting in February with members of People First, all of whom had experience of living in a group home. Some are now living independently. Although the group was smaller than we had aimed for – eight people – enthusiastic discussion produced a large amount of detailed material which formed the basis of the questionnaires.

Areas of discussion at that first meeting included:

- living with other people
- visitors/friends/families/neighbours
- privacy
- pets
- rotas/rules/rights
- having a job
- relating to staff
- organising leisure activities.

Three further sessions were held, involving other members of People First besides the two consultants, in the course of preparing the questionnaires.

Collecting the information

It was decided to use interviewing as the formal way of gathering information. We also spent time with the residents in all aspects of their lives – at home, at the day centre, and in their leisure activities, so we learnt a lot through observation and informal talk.

With the agreement of the interviewees concerned, we recorded five interviews.

Developing the questionnaires

In designing the questionnaires we thought about how to make them helpful both for us in asking the questions and for the residents to answer. For example: simple, clear language; subjects the residents would know about; enough space to be able to pick out each question easily; enough space to be able to write in the answers. We asked ourselves continually whether a question seemed to be a leading question or not and, if necessary, altered it.

Residents' questionnaires

Material from the consultation meeting with People First members was grouped into topic areas, and specific questions were then devised for each topic area. Obviously it was important to allow People First members' ideas to have priority in relation to what the questionnaire covered, but the topics they wanted to include were compared with other consumer-based material.[3,4]

The areas covered by the questionnaires were:

- where you lived before
- physical surroundings
- house rules/organisation
- privacy/trust (confidentiality)
- relationship with staff/support workers
- relationships with outside professionals
- relationships with residents
- solving problems
- money
- clothes
- visitors
- neighbours/acquaintances
- friends and relationships
- religion/spiritual/cultural
- how residents feel about themselves
- making your own decisions/taking responsibility for your life
- leisure/weekends/evenings
- visits out/getting out and about
- hobbies
- holidays
- education
- work/day centre
- relationships with staff
- relationships with clients/students
- getting a job

At the end of each group of questions on one topic, provision was made for comparing with where people had lived before, using the following method:

Very Good	Good	All Right	Bad	Very Bad
☐	☐	☐	☐	☐

When asking these 'comparison questions', we also used the following visual device. We did not keep a record of when this was used, but just used the card when it seemed necessary/helpful. Since the five faces equalled the number of boxes, it was easy to record an appropriate answer.

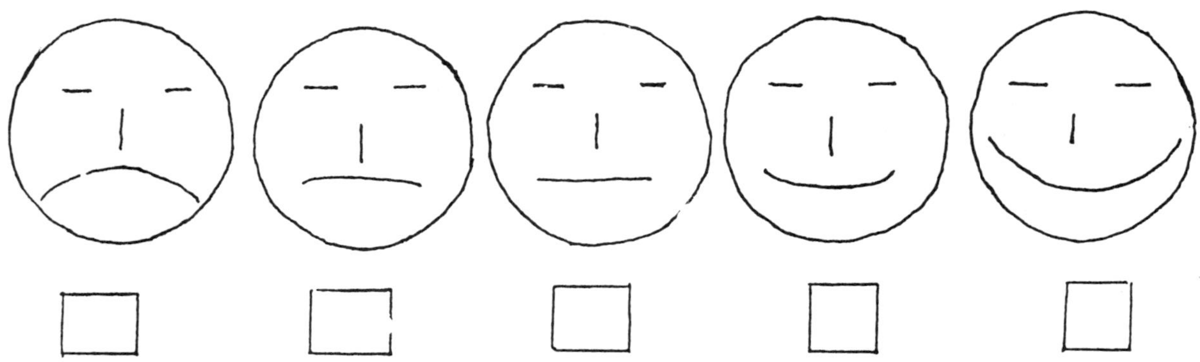

Staff questionnaires

We interviewed 11 staff – five working directly with the residents, two day centre managers, two hostel managers and one senior manager in charge of services.

The core ideas and important questions which People First wanted to ask staff were the same for everyone, but individual variations and additional questions had to be prepared to allow for differences in seniority of staff interviewed.

This resulted in three staff questionnaires. Samples are given in Part III of this book.

Preparing for the work

Simon and Joyce already had considerable skills which would help them with this work. Besides their own life experiences of services to people with learning difficulties, they both had experience of speaking in front of audiences – large and small – as speakers at conferences, trainers in workshops and leading small discussion groups. On a more individual level, they are skilled at making people feel at ease, helping people to speak up, and generally being friendly and getting on well with people.

Andrea had experience of helping people to express their own opinions and develop their own ideas without imposing her own or other people's opinions. This also means helping people to develop ways of working which suit them, at a pace which suits them. Andrea also had some relevant experience, having worked as a secretary in a market research firm for five years.

But undertaking a formal piece of work like this evaluation was new ground to us all. It was necessary to understand that an evaluation is much more than just chatting to people. It meant working in a very disciplined way. It meant concentrating for long periods at a time. We needed to do a lot of preparation work in order to do a thorough job.

In preparing for the interviews, we discussed the need not to ask leading questions, and what that meant. We talked about how it would be necessary to ask additional questions to those that were written down – if someone did not understand a question, or in order to get more information so that a question was answered properly, or in order to help somebody who was shy to speak up. We discussed – and practised using – helpful little words like Why? When? and How?

Interviewing

Simon and Joyce shared the interviewing. Sometimes they were both involved in interviewing one person; sometimes one or other did an interview on their own.

Joyce filled in the questionnaire and developed considerable skill in taking down accurate records of the answers. Simon did not do any writing, but was particularly skilled in asking supplementary, relevant questions. Andrea sat in on all interviews except one and also filled in a questionnaire.

Both consultants recorded additional impressions and opinions outside the interview situation – Joyce writing notes and Simon using a dictaphone. Five interviews were recorded.

The hand-written interviews were typed up and Joyce and Andrea's replies incorporated on the same sheet. (See sample overleaf.) It was interesting how often we found we had written exactly the same things, but also we sometimes chose to record different parts of a person's reply, which was useful when considering the results later.

Joyce and Simon became adept at explaining questions to people when necessary – perhaps when the question was too abstract or the person didn't seem to understand what was being asked. Sometimes they 'acted out' an example to help make it clearer.

ARE RESIDENTS INVOLVED IN MAKING DECISIONS ABOUT THE HOUSE?	YES ☐	NO ☐	DON'T KNOW ☐

AW: MOSTLY DECISIONS ABOUT PERSONAL DETAILS STILL.
CARPET COLOUR CHOSEN COLLECTIVELY.

JK: THEY HELPED TO PICK THE CARPETS & THE PAINT FOR THEIR BEDROOMS. ONE OF OUR RESIDENTS THAT CAME FROM HOME IS MORE INDEPENDENT. BY WASHING THEMSELVES AND DOING THINGS WHICH THEY DID NOT DO BEFORE.

ARE ANY DECISIONS MADE WITHOUT INVOLVING RESIDENTS?	YES ☐	NO ☐	DON'T KNOW ☐

AW: WE WOULD TRY AND EXPLAIN ABOUT DECISIONS.
EPILEPSY – WE HAVE TO MAKE DECISIONS ABOUT TAKING MEDICINE
DATES OF REVIEWS MIGHT BE CHANGED WITHOUT CONSULTING RESIDENTS.

JK: WE TRY TO EXPLAIN TO THE RESIDENTS. REVIEW: CLIENTS SIT IN AND IF THEY THINK OF SOMETHING THEY WANT PUT ON THE PAPER THEY CAN TELL THEM.

DO YOU HAVE A HOUSE MEETING WITH THE RESIDENTS?	YES ☐	NO ☐	DON'T KNOW ☐

AW: ON-GOING TALKING – NO SET TIME – NO SITTING DOWN TOGETHER. DO THEY GET A CHANCE FOR ONE-TO-ONE? YES.

JK: WE DON'T HAVE AN OFFICIAL MEETING, THEY JUST COME UP TO STAFF AND ASK IF THEY CAN HAVE A WORD WITH US.

HAVE YOU CHANGED ANYTHING THAT THE RESIDENTS ASKED FOR?	YES ☐	NO ☐	DON'T KNOW ☐

AW: CHANGED BATH ROUTINE

JK: SOME LIKE BATHS IN THE MORNING AND SOME AT NIGHT, BUT IT IS IMPORTANT THEY DO HAVE A BATH EVERY DAY.

HOW DO YOU INVOLVE PEOPLE IN PLANNING WHAT THEY WANT TO DO? (PERSONAL PLANS/REVIEWS/IPPS)

AW: HAVE A CHAT ABOUT IT

JK: REVIEW – INDEPENDENT CHAIRPERSON, RESIDENT, FAMILY/FRIEND, LINK WORKER AND KEY WORKER

The numbers game

- The average length of interview was one-and-a-half hours. The longest was two-and-a-half hours and the shortest half-an-hour.
- We did 19 interviews – seven residents, ten staff, and two family members.
- We made ten visits to places other than the two houses.
- We did over 600 miles of driving.
- The consultants put in 119 hours work each, the supporter 378 hours.

4 Results

Introduction

Results are given separately for each house.

1. We present a brief picture of who lives there and the sort of life they lead.
2. We give details about their answers to our questions and then give our own comments.
3. A chart sets out the results of the questions which compared life now to what it was like before.
4. To summarise the results we have used a way of looking at services known as 'the five accomplishments' – community presence, relationships, choice, competence, respect. More details about this are given at the beginning of that section.

What life is like for the people at Valley Road

The people at Valley Road

All three residents had previously lived at Hillside, a residential hostel where 25 people currently live, which until less than two years ago had been run on extremely out-of-date institutional lines.

None of the residents has any seriously handicapping physical or intellectual disabilities. The residents were:

Peter Weston – 43 – who has lived in hostels for most of his life. In Hillside for 22 years.

Helen Gordon – 69 – who had lived in Hillside for eight years. Before that she had been living with her sister after her mother had gone into a nursing home.

Mary Lewis – 58 – who had moved to Valley Road after 22 years at Hillside.

One resident has a full-time job as a cleaner. Life for the other two residents centres on the local day centre and activities associated with it. All three occasionally visit members of their immediate family. They have casual contacts with neighbours, e.g. say 'Hello' in the street. Their spare time activities mostly revolve around the house – watching TV, reading books, fixing electrical equipment, knitting and sewing.

One resident goes to a cookery class and two are involved in senior citizens' groups. Outings are to the social club attached to the day centre, the pub, an occasional visit to the cinema. Holidays have been at a variety of places in the UK, and one resident has been abroad.

Where they lived before

▲ *What was it like living in the hostel?*

▲ *What help did you get before leaving the hostel?*

▲ *Were you scared about leaving the hostel?*

▲ *What's it like living away from the hostel?*

All the residents said it was very good at the house compared with where they had lived before. 'I liked it but it got a bit noisy. I used to help other people – staff let me. It's lovely to be on your own, being in the house.'

'Quite liked it at Hillside. Very nice until one or two rough ones came there. But I wanted to get a home of my own. It seems to be a lot better. I miss one or two of my friends at Hillside, but I can always pop down to see them. I haven't been down a lot since I've been here.'

Consultants' comments

We felt that people are happy in the house – they get on well together and are, on the whole, content with the way things are. They are older – two being close to retiring age – and all have spent many years in institutions. They do not seem to expect a lot from life.

They take more responsibility for themselves and can look after themselves much more than the people in the other house. They act more as individuals – not so much as a group like in the other house.

We feel it took longer to get to know the people in this house. But as Joyce said, 'Every time we've gone back, they all seem to be more talkative and asking us "when are you coming again?" Both .... and .... seemed to open up to us more, because I said don't be afraid of speaking up, because what you tell us nobody else in the house will know. So she started talking to us about different things. She kept on talking when I was trying to ask another question. I could hardly get a word in, and that's a change!'

The house (physical surroundings)

▲ *Is the house what you imagined it to be?*

▲ *Would you like to improve the house (decorating, furniture, etc.)?*

▲ *Did you choose your furniture?*

▲ *Are you allowed to have pets?*

All the residents were very happy with the house as it is – only one small change about placing the furniture was mentioned.

They had all been to the house before moving in. One resident mentioned having seen another house as well 'but we liked this one straightaway'. Another comment was, '... was like in a daydream because she liked it that much.'

Consultants' comments

It is good that the house is an ordinary house which is similar to all the other houses around, so it doesn't stand out as being any different. However, we don't like the fact that it is right at the end of the housing estate. It is a confusing maze of streets to find it: even after several visits we still made mistakes getting there in the car. We realise that after a while you would get used to it if you lived there, but we think its situation might put off other people from going there – visitors, friends, etc.

We feel it is important that the places where people live are close to public transport, not only for the people who live there but to make it easier for other people to get there without having to ask someone to take them.

We think the house is a bit small for three adults – all leading their own lives. The kitchen is small, the bedrooms are very small – particularly since they are the only private place each person has to keep all their personal things. The house is nicely decorated and furnished but we were surprised to see that there were no lampshades on the ceiling lights – a house needs lampshades in it to feel really homely.

Rules and regulations

House rules/organisation

▲ *How do you organise this? (cooking, cleaning, taking turns for the bathroom)*

▲ *Do you ever sit down together for a meal?*

▲ *Do you have a residents' committee/house meeting?*

There is a rota for cooking but people take turns to do the cleaning – 'whoever is around and sees it needs to be done'. Each person looks after his/her own bedroom.

Having only one toilet was mentioned as being 'a bit of a problem'.

They don't have a regular 'house meeting' – only if a problem crops up.

Consultants' comments

The arrangements for cooking and cleaning seemed to work well – except occasionally when the 'man of the house doesn't pull his weight'! We feel that having a regular meeting would be a good idea because it helps prevent problems arising in the first place.

Money

▲ *Do you handle your own money?*

▲ *Do you understand the value of money? (Paying rent/budgeting/bills/personal money)*

▲ *Do you cash your own benefit book?*

All residents understand coinage. One person who is working full time and is not on benefits looks after his own money. The other two residents only look after their own pocket/personal money which they collect each week from Hillside. They do not handle rent or other larger amounts of money independently. Staff give them money for housekeeping each week.

Medication

▲ *Are you responsible for taking your own medication?*

The two residents who need medication go each week to the hostel to collect a week's supply. When asked why they had to do this every week, one resident said, 'They said I'd take too much – I wouldn't. I lost a cousin from an overdose – I'm careful. I think they should give me a chance to prove I can do it.'

Consultants' comments

We feel that this arrangement of having to go back to the hostel every week for money and medication does not help them to get away from the 'institutional feeling' – to get more of a feeling of being independent. It's just as though they were still there – as if the staff didn't trust them. They'll never feel free if these practices aren't stopped.

We think there should be one staff person in charge of the budget and tablets who would go to the house and help the residents learn to manage these things themselves. They have to learn to put so much away each week for rent, so much for holidays, so much for food etc. They should have their own book and staff should teach them to go to the post office and draw the money out themselves. They can still go to the hostel to see friends, but they wouldn't feel that they had to go, even if they didn't want to.

Getting on with staff

- ▲ *Were the staff in the house chosen by you?*
- ▲ *Do you get on with the staff?*
- ▲ *How do staff help you?*

One resident said she got on well with staff. Other comments were 'fairly well', 'sometimes – sometimes not'.

Names of staff who might come to the house were discussed with the residents beforehand. One resident mentioned a preference for a member of staff who wasn't chosen to work in the house.

At first staff slept in – now they just come a few times during the week. Saturday, Sunday and Tuesday were stated as being the days. One resident said, 'We like it better when they're not here. But we get to speak by phone. We like them as long as they behave alright!' One resident had asked for them to leave but another had realised they needed them for help with 'reading and writing'.

Consultants' comments

We felt that staff had done well in the nine months since the people had moved in. It is good that they have 'backed away' from living in as they had at first, to just being there on Saturday, Sunday and Tuesday.

Getting on with other residents

- ▲ *Do you get on well with each other? (arguments, atmosphere)*
- ▲ *Did you know each other before you moved into the house?*
- ▲ *Do the other people in the house understand about privacy?*
- ▲ *Do you trust one another?*

All the residents knew each other before moving into the house. They get on with each other well most of the time. There has been the occasional argument, but it was soon made up.

Two residents said they did trust the others in the house. The third resident said, 'not entirely'. Although they all said they understood about privacy, there was some doubt in our minds as to whether this was actually true. One example of a resident entering a room without knocking was told to us. A similar incident happened while we were interviewing one of the residents.

We talked about locks on bedroom and bathroom doors. The lock on the bathroom door was not working. One resident said that staff had said it was dangerous to have a lock. We know that if a person is taken ill, or has a fit, it is important that people can get in to help, but we feel that privacy is important and there are other ways of thinking about this. For example, a notice to hang on the bathroom door or fit a lock which can be opened from outside in an emergency.

We also talked about locks on bedroom doors. People First members feel it is important to be able to lock your own bedroom door. There are no locks on the bedroom doors at Valley Road. Two residents said they would like one. One resident was waiting for her bedroom door catch to be fixed.

Consultants' comments

We feel that the people in this house live more as individuals – they keep themselves to themselves – perhaps because they are older. We noticed that when the staff were there, the residents seemed to 'hand over' responsibility to them again – as if they were back in the institution. We think it is important that staff work with residents one-to-one – not as a group – to help get over this institutional feeling and get away from the 'us' and 'them' feeling.

Solving problems

- ▲ *If you have a problem, who do you go and see?*
- ▲ *Does your problem get solved?*

When asked who they would go to for help with solving problems, all residents mentioned family members, house staff or the hostel manager. When asked what they would do if this didn't solve the problem, they were unable to answer.

Consultants' comments

One of the aims of these questions was to find out if the residents knew and understood about complaints procedures. Hillingdon has a very detailed, clearly documented complaints procedure. When we asked specifically about the complaints procedure, they didn't seem to understand the term or know about it. A senior staff person told us that the complaints procedure had been explained to them but she doubted if they really understood it.

How residents feel about themselves

- ▲ *Do you find it difficult to ask for help?*
- ▲ *Do you feel more confident?*
- ▲ *Can you say 'No'? (Being assertive)*

Making your own decisions/taking responsibility for your life

- ▲ *Can you go out when you want to?*
- ▲ *Can you come back when you want to?*
- ▲ *Can you have a bath/cup of tea when you want to?*
- ▲ *Can you go to the pub on your own?*
- ▲ *Do you have your own front door key?*

- ▲ *Do you have your own bedroom door key?*
- ▲ *Do you choose what you wear?*
- ▲ *Do you go out and buy your own clothes?*

All the residents said that this part of their lives was very good compared to where they had lived before. They were more confident and could speak up for themselves much more now. We felt that they were very pleased to say this. 'There was always staff around (at the hostel) telling you what to do. I can just do what I want now.'

When they go out, they tell a staff person and they tell them when they come back. We would suggest that people leave a note for the other residents when they go out, saying when they'll be back. Then they would not have to tell staff every time.

Friends and relationships

- ▲ *Do you find it easy to make friends?*
- ▲ *Who are your friends?*
- ▲ *Where did you meet them?*
- ▲ *Do you have a special friend?*
- ▲ *Would you like to tell us more about your friends?*

One resident said friends were people at work. The other two residents said staff or people at the day centre or the hostel were their friends.

Consultants' comments

Making friends is difficult to help with because you have to introduce people to each other – you can't make friends for other people. We feel staff should take people to places where there are people who might become friends. But it is important that staff support people properly in this. The following account of Joyce's experience of going to a lunch club with one of the ladies from Valley Road illustrates this point. This lunch club for elderly people is organised at a local community centre. A group of eight from Ford Lane day centre attend every week. They all sit together at the one table. On this occasion Joyce was meant to be one of the eight but found she had to sit at a separate table.

> *At 12.30 Andrea and Simon stayed at the Centre to interview Kay the Boss, while I went with Helen to a lunch club for my dinner. I really was hungry. When I went in and sat down I was just going to enjoy my dinner, when a lady came up to me and asked me 'How did you get in here?' When I tried to explain I was with Helen and seven others she just kept on asking me or saying 'I'm not bothered who you are with, I want to know how you got in'. I told her Kay had phoned to explain, but she said nobody had phoned her up. When I said 'I'll leave if you want', she said 'no, sit down and have your dinner'. With all the talking and so on, my dinner was cold, but I was that hungry I ate it.*
>
> *Then when everyone had finished their dinner they all got up and left, and there was just the seven of us left there. I asked Helen what time did they usually*

come for her and the others. She said 1.30, so we went outside for half an hour in the cold. Then a mini bus came to take us back to the Centre.

Neighbours and acquaintances

- ▲ *Do you get on with your neighbours?*
- ▲ *How do other people treat you? (patronising, with respect?)*

Neighbours say 'hello' in the street. One once offered a lift to the main road and another offered the loan of garden tools. One helped when a resident was shut out of the house. They have not been into any neighbours' houses and have not invited them into theirs. One resident was invited to a child's party – took a present but didn't stay.

Consultants' comments

We do not feel this is very much contact with neighbours but we have no way of comparing it with what happens between other homes on the estate. It would be good to see what happens between them when the residents are outside and the neighbours are outside.

Visitors

Although residents are allowed to have visitors whenever they want, they did not speak of having any visitors other than staff or family. If they had more friends, they could ask them to visit. Staff could introduce them to their own friends.

Family

One resident visits her sister once a month. The other two residents see family members occasionally. During the evaluation all three residents had visits to their families. We tried to make arrangements to talk to members of each resident's family, but it became clear that the residents were not really keen on the idea and we respected their wishes.

Daytime activities

Peter has a full-time job as a cleaner. The two ladies go to the day centre five days a week. Of these, one said she liked going there – it was 'something to do'; the other felt 'half and half' about it. She liked the work in the workshop (making up plastic book covers) but didn't like it when 'people get at me'. What she liked best about it was 'getting the money'.

Both ladies have done work experience and both would like a proper job. One had tried to get herself a job at the local Express Dairy but had been told she was too old. Staff at the centre had got her a job at a playgroup but this had been stopped because it was thought to be too much for her.

Consultants' comments

We didn't feel that this lady, in particular, liked being at Ford Lane centre. We felt that both ladies would have been better off at Greenbank.

Our report on Ford Lane is included later in this report.

Leisure and hobbies

Peter mostly spends his evenings in the house watching TV, reading or fixing things (e.g. electrical things/wireless). He occasionally goes to the pub. One of the ladies spends her evenings at home, watching TV, playing tapes, looking after her budgerigars; the other has a cookery class one evening and goes to a Gateway Club another night.

Consultants' comments

We would like the residents to have much more opportunity to go to ordinary places in the community and do ordinary things. We feel that they will need a lot more help and encouragement from staff to do this.

The residents don't seem to have many hobbies – one resident mentioned going to the library but stopped because she couldn't get the books back on time. We would like to see her given more help with this – e.g. writing in her diary the day the books have to go back. The residents should have more help to go to evening classes.

We feel that particularly for two of them, there is too much routine in their lives – they do the same things every week and most of the things they do are connected with services. We would like to see staff introduce them to more different things.

Contact with other professionals

When asked whether they had chosen their own GP, one resident said 'No' and two said 'Yes'. One lady said she found it strange at first going to the doctor (the doctor had come in to the hostel) but liked it now. The other lady said she found it difficult to understand her Indian doctor. She was annoyed that staff wouldn't let her go to the doctor on her own.

Support for the house

When the house first opened, several staff were involved, but it was realised that too many different people were going to the house. Now just two staff help the residents. We interviewed both of them.

One of the staff had been 'rota'd' to the house from the hostel, where she had worked for 17 months. She had a week's induction course and had been on a personal relationships course and a course on benefits. Her past experience was as a housewife and mother. The other staff member had worked with elderly people for 12 years before coming to the house. When asked about the aims of the house they said:

> *'To help them achieve and get what they want from life. To take care of their own finances. To extend what they are already doing.'*

'I'd like people to be independent – able to mix in the community more than at present. They are quite dependent on the hostel for going out. Transport is a problem.'

What the staff liked best about the job was working with a smaller group and seeing individual people gain more skills: 'It's great to see their achievements.' 'There's more consistency at Valley Road. You can see it growing into something – you can see the good things and the bad things better.'

One of the things least liked about the job was the 'red tape you have to go through to get anything done'. It was hoped this situation would improve once a proposed transfer of the management of the house to a housing association was achieved.

The good and bad points about working on your own were also mentioned. 'If there is a problem, at (the hostel) you can go and talk to someone about it. You can't in the smaller house. In a way that's good, because it makes you think more about what you are doing.'

They do reviews with each resident once a year – 'more often if they ask for them'.

Consultants' comments

The staff are very nice people but we feel they should 'push' the residents more. They said they wanted people to be more independent and do more ordinary things in the community but they didn't seem to have many ideas about how to do this. We like the idea one of the staff mentioned of having a 'training' day during the week to do chores so that the residents could do more 'fun' things at the weekend.

What life is like for the people at Prince Street

The people at Prince Street

Four men live in this house. Three had previously lived at Holly Grange, a hostel where 18 people are currently living. The hostel has been running for ten years.

Paul Smith – 26 – had lived at Holly Grange for eight years. Before that he had been in a children's home after leaving his family home. Paul is gradually learning to communicate more and increase his spoken vocabulary. He is proud to show you what he is learning using letter and number cards.

John McLean – 42 – had lived at Holly Grange for seven years. Prior to that, he lived with his grandmother. John has no seriously handicapping physical or intellectual disabilities.

Stephen Jones – 38 – lived with his mother before moving to Prince Street, but had been to Holly Grange for short stays. Stephen's life has been restricted because of very severe epilepsy.

Michael Williams – 19 – had lived with his family until three years ago when he moved to Holly Grange. Michael has a severe hearing disability and uses sign language to communicate.

Two residents attend a day centre five days a week, one resident has a specially designed individual day service, and the fourth resident is involved in a YTS scheme and attends college two days a week. All residents have regular and frequent contact with close family. They have no significant contact with neighbours.

They are involved in a range of club-type social activities, all except one of these having some link with special services – e.g. Gateway Club, woodwork class, PHAB Club, social club at the day centre. The one non-service-based group activity is a club for people who are hard of hearing, which one resident attends. Other outings on a more individual basis are to the pub, visits to families of the staff, sightseeing.

Where they lived before

- ▲ *What was it like living in the hostel?*
- ▲ *What help did you get before leaving the hostel?*
- ▲ *Were you scared about leaving the hostel?*
- ▲ *What's it like living away from the hostel?*

Two out of the four residents liked it better in the house than the hostel: 'Good fun living here. Going to work in the morning and coming back in the car instead of the coach.' One resident liked the hostel better. The fourth resident had lived at home before moving to the house and said he liked it as much as living at home: 'I like it. I enjoy it'.

Consultants' comments

This is a very happy, caring house. We felt at ease right from the start. Simon commented: 'The first impression that I got from this house was when we got there, they welcomed us with open arms. It was a nice atmosphere in the house – it was a great house. I really enjoyed looking around the bungalow. One of the residents showed us his bedroom and what pictures he had on the wall, photographs and so on, and that was a nice welcome.'

The house (physical surroundings)

- ▲ *Is the house what you imagined it to be?*
- ▲ *Would you like to improve the house? (decorating, furniture, etc.)*
- ▲ *Did you choose your furniture?*
- ▲ *Are you allowed to have pets?*

All the residents liked the house and didn't want to make any changes. Even the resident who preferred being in the hostel 'likes his blue bedroom at Prince Street better'. The residents were not involved in choosing the house. They all chose their own bedroom furniture and were involved in other decisions like choosing the carpeting for the house. Three out of the four residents would like a cat as a pet. The fourth resident's comment was: 'I'm not mad about pets. If I had some, I'd only have to feed them'.

Consultants' comments

We liked the fact that it was an ordinary house which looked the same as others in the street. One of us didn't like the fact that it was – like the other house – in a corner at the end of the street – 'Just as if they want to keep people out of the way'.

There is a nice lot of space in this house. The decorations and furniture are of a high standard.

Rules and regulations

House rules/organisation

- ▲ *How do you organise this? (cooking, cleaning, taking turns for the bathroom)*
- ▲ *Do you ever sit down together for a meal?*
- ▲ *Do you have a residents' committee/house meeting?*

There are no rotas for cleaning or cooking. All residents give a hand with these jobs according to their skills. All can do simple things like making a drink or making toast. One resident does all his own washing, pegging out and ironing. Another can do the hoovering and has washed up 'about a 100 times!'. Staff told us that, as a result of our visits, this man had gained the confidence to object to this and get that situation changed.

They do not have a house meeting – just talk about things informally, as the need arises.

Money

- ▲ *Do you handle your own money?*
- ▲ *Do you understand the value of money? (paying rent/budgeting/bills/personal money)*
- ▲ *Do you cash your own benefit book?*

Three of the residents understand coinage and look after their own personal spending money. Staff handle everything else to do with money. They try and involve residents wherever possible, e.g. signing the cheque for rent.

Medication

- ▲ *Are you responsible for taking your own medication?*

Staff make sure that residents take their medication – none of the residents can manage this on his own yet.

Consultants' comments

All the people in this house still need a lot of help from staff. It was good to see how they were helping without imposing a lot of rules and regulations.

Getting on with staff

- ▲ *Were the staff in the house chosen by you?*
- ▲ *Do you get on with the staff?*
- ▲ *How do staff help you?*
- ▲ *When are staff in the house?*

All the residents knew the staff before they moved into the house. They all said they get on well with the staff. When asked how staff help them, they said things like:

> 'Take me out to pub and Windsor Castle.'
> 'Help me to get to work on time.'
> 'When I feel unhappy.'
> 'Help me to do my cuffs up. I couldn't do that before.'
> 'Talk to me like a man.'

Consultants' comments

We felt that the staff worked very well with the residents. There was a very easy, relaxed atmosphere in the house. They joked and laughed with each other a lot. One staff person said: 'We get over little ups and downs very quickly because all of the residents and the staff have a sense of humour.'

Getting on with the other residents

- ▲ *Do you get on well with each other? (arguments, 'atmosphere')*
- ▲ *Did you know each other before you moved into the house?*

All the residents had known each other before they moved. Three said they got on well with the other residents.

The fourth man, when asked if he had a friend in the house, said 'No'. Staff told us they felt this was because there were more people at the hostel whom he could have some sort of contact with, despite his communication difficulties.

One man had a clear understanding about privacy and trust. We were not sure about the answers from the other residents because of the abstract nature of the questions.

Consultants' comments

As far as we could tell from our visits, all the residents got on well with each other. They were living together happily without necessarily being close friends with each other.

Solving problems

- ▲ *If you have a problem, who do you go and see?*
- ▲ *Does your problem get solved?*

When asked who they would go to for help with a problem, three people said staff or close family. The fourth person didn't seem to have any problems and found the question amusing: 'I'll do it myself!'

Consultants' comments

Although we gave the residents examples of what we meant by a problem, we found it difficult to help them answer these questions in any detail. But, apart from the example mentioned earlier of the man who complained about doing too much washing up, we did not get the impression that the residents wanted to complain about things.

How residents feel about themselves

- ▲ *Do you find it difficult to ask for help?*
- ▲ *Do you feel more confident?*
- ▲ *Can you say 'no'? (being assertive)*

The abstract nature of these questions and the communication problems made it difficult for us to get answers to all the questions in this section from all of the residents. However, we feel that two of the residents understood the questions. Both answered 'yes' to the questions about being more confident and assertive. When asked if they found it difficult to ask for help, one said 'no' and the other said 'sometimes'.

Making your own decisions/taking responsibility for your life

- ▲ *Can you go out when you want to?*
- ▲ *Can you come back when you want to?*
- ▲ *Can you have a bath/cup of tea when you want to?*
- ▲ *Can you go to the pub on your own?*
- ▲ *Do you have your own front door key?*
- ▲ *Do you have your own bedroom door key?*
- ▲ *Do you choose what you wear?*
- ▲ *Do you go out and buy your own clothes?*

One man can go out on his own and use public transport. Another can go to the local shops, but 'I tell staff before I go'. (At the hostel, this man would only go 'across the road'.) The other two men do not go out without someone going with them. All the men have their own front door key but no bedroom door keys.

All can and do make decisions for themselves in the house, e.g. have a bath, make a cup of tea.

Staff told us that they felt all four men had gained in confidence and skills since they had moved, e.g. 'John is a lot more organised. Michael is more independent. Paul has improved greatly – wants to communicate – is much calmer.'

Consultants' comments

The people in this house have only been there four months – they still need a lot of help from staff. They still have a lot of skills to learn. We would be very interested to see what progress they have made if we visited them again in a year from now.

Friends and relationships

- ▲ *Do you find it easy to make friends?*
- ▲ *Who are your friends?*
- ▲ *Where did you meet them?*
- ▲ *Do you have a special friend?*
- ▲ *Would you like to tell us more about your friends?*

For all the residents, friends meant staff, people in the house or from the day centre, and people in the street – 'they go along the road but I don't know their names'.

Having to rely on signing to communicate made it particularly difficult for one young man to make friends. A friend from the day centre had been invited for the day but she didn't come again. As one staff member said: 'There is a big difference between casual meetings at the day centre and spending six hours together.'

Staff at Prince Street are very aware that the residents don't have many friends and are thinking hard about how to change this. We liked their idea of trying to get advocates who would take the residents out, introduce them to different people and so help them to make friends.

Neighbours and acquaintances

▲ *Do you get on with your neighbours?*

▲ *How do other people treat you? (patronising, with respect?)*

All residents said they got on with their neighbours. They did not have much to say about people met on a casual basis – but what they did say was positive, e.g. 'Bloke in the pub bought me a drink'.

Staff told us that there was not much contact with neighbours. They say 'hello' in the street. The only actual contact has been over difficulties about use of the parking space outside the house. As one staff member put it: 'Everyone is an island in this street'.

Visitors

The residents can have visitors whenever they want but, as with the other house, we did not get the impression that they had many visitors other than staff and family.

Family

All the residents have frequent contact with their families. One resident goes home most weekends and another visits his grandmother every Saturday. The other two men see their families approximately once a fortnight. Staff told us that one mother came much more often to the house than she had to the hostel: 'It took much more organising at [the hostel]'. On the other hand, one of the residents said 'Nan can't visit me now – too far away'.

We were only able to interview two members of the residents' families – Stephen's mother and John's grandmother. Both were very happy about Stephen and John moving to Prince Street.

'It's ideal for Stephen. I used to worry about what would happen to him when I go.'

'I was eager for John to move. I wanted him to move from Holly Grange.' John's grandmother was disappointed he didn't have his own bedroom – 'appropriate for someone his age' – otherwise she was pleased.

Both ladies were very pleased with the progress the men had made: 'He's getting more independent – Meg [support worker] is bringing him out very well. He looks well – slimmer.'

'John likes it. I want him to be happy.'

Changes they would like to see in the future were: 'Like to see his speech improve'; 'Job with more money'; '. . . more use of words like "please" and "thank you": I've noticed less of these since he went to the house!'

We asked them if they went to meetings with Stephen and John at the day centre and/or at the house. They both said – 'No'. One said: 'I know what is happening through asking . . . I'm happy without having a meeting'.

Both ladies got on well with the staff in the house and had frequent contact with them.

Daytime activities

Two men attend Greenbank day centre five days a week. One said he liked the centre and wanted to stay there. He didn't want a job outside the centre. We were not able to interview the other man about the centre because of the communication difficulties. We spent a day with them at the Centre and our report is included later in this section.

One man has a specially-designed individual day service. Each day he goes to the house of the lady who is employed to support him and help him learn new skills. They go shopping, do gardening, watch TV, go out to the pub. When asked if he liked this he said, 'It's all right, I suppose'. When asked if he'd like a proper job he said, 'Yes!!' with great enthusiasm. This man attends a literacy class at an adult education college one morning a week.

The fourth man goes twice a week to a college for people with learning disabilities, and attends a YTS course the other three days. At the college he learns signing, literacy skills, computing and woodwork. His support worker had some doubts about the value of the YTS course since no-one there could do signing. She was hoping he would be able to go full-time to the college for people with hearing disabilities.

Leisure and hobbies

The things people do in their spare time include listening to music, gardening, woodwork, going to the pub, to the pictures, sightseeing. They are involved in five different clubs held mostly in the evenings.

Hobbies people said they would like to do in the future included basketwork and pottery.

Consultants' comments

We thought the number of different activities that people were involved in was very good but we were very aware of the amount of time and energy spent by staff in, as one put it, 'being a taxi service' for all these activities. It was good to hear, at the feedback meeting, that they have started to use volunteer drivers, and that with the longer, warmer days, they are able to spend more time on teaching people to travel on public transport.

All but one of the clubs people go to have some connection with services. We hope that staff keep on trying to find ways of linking the residents with people and places in the 'ordinary community'.

Contact with other professionals

None of the residents chose their own GP. Everyone at the hostel where the Prince Street residents had come from have the same GP.

A speech therapist had been employed for 12 weeks, to train staff to help the young man who is just learning to speak. This had worked well, but funding had now come to an end and the staff member most concerned had left, so progress had been interrupted.

Support for the house

Four staff are helping the residents. There is always at least one staff member on duty throughout the day and night. Staff are gradually increasing the time people can be left on their own – for example, for one man it has increased from five minutes to fifteen minutes; for another it is up to half-an-hour at a time.

We interviewed three of the staff. The fourth member of staff left during the beginning of our interviewing period and we were unable to fit in a time to talk to him. The post was not filled until after the evaluation was over.

The three staff we interviewed had all worked at the hostel with the four residents; the head of the house had known them there for five years.

When asked about their past experience, staff said things like:

- bringing up a family;
- working in an old people's home;
- voluntary work with people with learning difficulties;
- catering.

The only formal qualification mentioned was one person who had training in signing and counselling.

When asked about the aims of the house they said:

- being a happy home;
- to promote independence;
- to improve the quality of life for the people here.

What they all liked best about the job was the opportunity to spend more time with each resident because of the small group. 'It's possible to do things here that you can't do in the larger hostel.' 'You can see your plans through.'

When asked what they liked least, they mentioned 'more stress – trying to get everything done'; 'times when you feel isolated [from other workers]'; 'paperwork'. One of the good things mentioned was 'marvellous support from my supervisor'.

For each resident they hold a formal review annually and do reports every three months.

Consultants' comments

Staff have done well in helping people gain more skills – there is more going on in that house to encourage new skills.

They have done well in getting people involved in the 'ordinary world'. Two of the residents still spend a lot of their time in activities run by social services. But of the other two – one young man will be going to college full-time in September, and the fourth man is hoping to get a job soon.

More members of staff should learn signing to help the man with hearing disability to communicate better.

More travel training is needed to enable the residents to get about on public transport and not have to rely on staff to take them everywhere.

Is life better now?

Residents' comparisons with where they used to live

As explained earlier, questions were grouped under various topic headings. After each group of questions we asked residents how that area of their life compared with where they had lived before.

For example, after the questions about house rules and organisation (cooking, cleaning, bath routines, etc.) we asked them to choose one of five answers (shown on the chart) which would best describe how rules in the house compared with rules in the hostel. Sometimes we used the five 'sad-to-happy' faces to help people answer these questions.

The following charts give the results of these comparisons. Some explanation is needed about the last column:

Not applicable: in some instances it was not possible to make a comparison – e.g. some people had not yet been on a holiday since living in the house, so couldn't compare with where they had lived before.

Not answered: in relation to Prince Street, this column also reflects the difficulties we had with getting answers in the more abstract topic areas, and the difficulties of communicating with some of the residents. However, we were often able to get further information through chatting informally, or from what staff told us.

Valley Road

Compared with where you lived before	VERY GOOD	GOOD	*ALL RT. NO DIFF.	BAD	VERY BAD	**DK N/AP N/AN
WHERE YOU LIVED BEFORE (overall comparison)	✓✓✓					
THE HOUSE	✓✓	✓				
HOUSE RULES	✓✓		✓			
PRIVACY	✓		✓✓			
RELATIONSHIP WITH STAFF	✓	✓	✓			
RELATIONSHIP WITH OTHER PROFESSIONALS	✓		✓✓			
RELATIONSHIP WITH RESIDENTS	✓	✓	✓			
SOLVING PROBLEMS	✓		✓✓			
MONEY		✓	✓✓			
CLOTHES	✓✓		✓			
NEIGHBOURS		✓✓	✓			
FRIENDS		✓	✓			✓
RELIGION/ OTHER CULTURES	✓		✓✓			
VISITORS	✓		✓✓			
HOW RESIDENTS FEEL ABOUT THEMSELVES	✓✓✓					
MAKING YOUR OWN DECISIONS	✓✓					✓
VISITS OUT	✓		✓✓			
HOBBIES			✓✓			✓
HOLIDAYS						✓✓✓
EDUCATION						✓✓✓

*All Rt. = All right

No Diff. = No difference

**DK = Don't know

N/AP = Not applicable

N/AB = Not answered

Prince Street

Compared with where you lived before	VERY GOOD	GOOD	*ALL RT. NO DIFF.	BAD	VERY BAD	**DK N/AP N/AN
WHERE YOU LIVED BEFORE (overall comparison)	✓	✓	✓		✓	
THE HOUSE	✓	✓	✓			✓
HOUSE RULES	✓✓		✓			✓
PRIVACY	✓	✓	✓			✓
RELATIONSHIP WITH STAFF	✓		✓			✓✓
RELATIONSHIP WITH OTHER PROFESSIONALS			✓			✓✓✓
RELATIONSHIP WITH RESIDENTS			✓✓			✓✓
SOLVING PROBLEMS			✓✓	✓		✓
MONEY		✓	✓✓✓			
CLOTHES	✓		✓✓✓			
NEIGHBOURS	✓	✓	✓			✓
FRIENDS			✓✓	✓		✓
RELIGION/ OTHER CULTURES						✓✓✓✓
VISITORS	✓		✓✓	✓		
HOW RESIDENTS FEEL ABOUT THEMSELVES		✓✓	✓			✓
MAKING YOUR OWN DECISIONS		✓	✓✓			✓
VISITS OUT		✓				✓✓✓
HOBBIES		✓				✓✓✓
HOLIDAYS			✓			✓✓✓
EDUCATION			✓			✓✓✓

*All Rt. = All right

No Diff. = No difference

**DK = Don't know

N/AP = Not applicable

N/AB = Not answered

Summary of results

In order to give a summary of the results, we have adapted a way of looking at people's lives which was developed by John O'Brien, an American who works for better lives for people with learning difficulties.[5] He identified five important things to look for in people's lives in judging whether services are doing a good job. The IDC booklet *Pursuing Quality*[6] describes these as follows:

1. **Community presence.** People with learning difficulties have the right to spend their time in the community, not segregated in residential, day or leisure facilities which keep them apart from other members of society.

2. **Relationships.** Living in the community is not enough. People also need help and encouragement to mix with other non-handicapped people in the course of their daily lives. We should be creating opportunities for people to form valued relationships at home, at work, in education and in community and leisure activities.

3. **Choice.** An important feature of the quality of life is the degree of choice that people can exercise. This can apply to small, everyday matters like what to wear or what to eat, and to major life decisions like who to live with or where to work. A high quality service will give priority to enhancing the choices available to people and to protecting their human rights generally.

4. **Competence.** In order for people with learning difficulties to live a full and rewarding life in their local community, many will require help in experiencing a growing ability to perform useful and meaningful activities with whatever assistance is required. This increase in competence should be directly relevant to people's life situations, helping them to develop relationships and achieve greater choice and independence.

5. **Respect.** People with learning difficulties often have an undeserved bad reputation and are seen and treated as second-class citizens. Services can play an important part in helping people to be seen and treated with the same status as other valued members of the community.

We looked at all five aspects when thinking about the people in the two houses. In the end, we decided to leave out the last area – respect. We felt we couldn't make a judgment here because during our two weeks at the house there were not enough opportunities to observe people interacting with ordinary members of the public.

The table below gives an overall view of how we feel services are helping the people in the two houses so far. We have just put it very simply, using + and −. But a + doesn't mean that everything is good, and a − doesn't mean that everything is bad! We realise that people have not been living in the houses very long and staff are only just beginning to be able to help people with some parts of their lives.

Following on from the table, we talk more about what progress we feel has been made.

	VALLEY ROAD			PRINCE STREET		
	At home (The Houses)	**Daytime** (working hours)	**Leisure**	**At home** (The houses)	**Daytime** (working hours)	**Leisure**
Community presence	+	–	–	+	+	–
Relationships	–	–	–	–	–	–
Choice	+	–	–	+	–	+
Competence	+	–	–	+	–	+

Community presence

The houses

Both houses score well here. The residents are living in houses which are like other homes around them and are in ordinary streets. In their new homes, the residents are 'in the community'.

Daytime living (working hours)

In Valley Road, one person has a full-time job, so is 'in the community', but the other two people go to the day centre five days a week.

We felt that Prince Street scored 50/50 on this. Although two people still go to the day centre, the other two have been spending their daytime hours mostly away from social services settings. Of these, one will be going to college full-time in September and steps have been taken to help the fourth man get a job.

Leisure

Neither house scores well. All the residents still rely on leisure activities which are linked to services. All except one of the clubs are run by service providers. Residents do go to the pub – but that is with a member of staff.

Relationships

Neither house scored well. Most of the people the residents come into contact with, apart from their families, are other people with disabilities or people who are paid to be with them. We felt that staff at Prince Street were very aware of this and were really trying to work out ways to change this situation.

Choice

All the residents get lots of small choices in their lives – mainly within their own homes, e.g. choosing clothes, food, bedtimes. They get very few large choices, e.g. alternatives to going to a day centre. Residents at Prince Street had more choice about what to do in their spare time, even though most of the choices were within services.

Competence

Again, in their own homes, all the residents are getting help to learn new skills. But away from the houses the picture is not so good. Neither house scores well in the areas of daytime activities or leisure, though there is more going on at Prince Street to provide opportunities for learning new skills. It is difficult for staff at Valley Road because of the people being much older and their experience of having spent many years in the hostel. People who have been institutionalised for a long time fall into a rut – you can't climb out of that rut, without a lot of help. Staff need training to know how best to help people.

Reports on the day centres

Ford Lane Centre

Report by Joyce Kershaw

I noticed when we arrived there was no-one there to help us. We did not have to sign a register like we did at Greenbank. Also the atmosphere when we walked in, and in the rooms, they smelt musty. I noticed a young man sitting in the corner of the room and he was still there when we left at 3.45, and we arrived at the centre at 9.30 a.m.

We asked to see Helen, and the Manager said we could use her office. We asked Helen the questions but there were a few she did not want to answer or could not. At 12.30 Andrea and Simon stayed at the centre to interview Kay, the Boss, while I went with Helen to the lunch club for my dinner. I really was hungry. When I went in and sat down I was just going to enjoy my dinner, when a lady came up to me and asked me 'How did you get in here?' When I tried to explain I was with Helen and seven others she just kept on asking me or saying 'I'm not bothered who you are with, I want to know how you got in'. I told her Kay had phoned to explain, but she said nobody had phoned her up. When I said 'I'll leave if you want', she said 'no, sit down and have your dinner'. With all the talking and so on, my dinner was cold, but I was that hungry I ate it.

Then when everyone had finished their dinner they all got up and left, and there was just the seven of us left there. I asked Helen what time did they usually come for her and the others. She said 1.30, so we went outside for half an hour in the cold. Then a mini bus came to take us back to the centre.

When I got back Andrea and Simon had finished their interview with Kay. We went and got a drink out of a machine. I went to the toilet and found a young lady sat on the seat with her legs crossed and would not come out, so I went and told one of the staff and she got her out, then had to start dressing her, so I came out. When I went back another girl threw a tea towel down the toilet and tried to flush it.

I don't think it was my day today!

In a clients' meeting just before we left they were asking for more staff. I think they could do with some as well. Also I noticed early on that there was only one ambulance box and that was in Kay's office.

Helen said she did some knitting at the centre. But Mary was rolling plastic for plastic files like we saw when we went to Greenbank day centre. Most of the people there just did what they wanted – just walked about – talking loudly – not bothering what they did.

I saw three people walking about in their bare feet. The staff didn't seem to notice.

They didn't seem to have any emotions for each other. I didn't notice anyone with their arms around their girlfriend, or talking to a special friend in the nice quiet way that they did at the other centre.

The furniture was old, and all the paint outside was coming off. In fact, to tell the truth, it was dirty and old and too small for all the people that was there. I have not seen a centre like it before. I know if I had a child with learning difficulty, I would not let him or her go to that centre.

It was very noisy, too. I don't know whether the staff were not bothered, but it seemed to me that Helen and Mary would be better off at the other centre. Helen said she liked it quiet; that is why she liked the house better than the home she used to live in, because there it was very noisy. Helen seemed to be more cheerful today, more talkative than when we first went to see her.

Recommendations

I think that the Ford Lane Centre could do with a few more staff, so Kay could get on with her boss's job, instead of having to keep getting up and going to see about things all the time. If she had two deputy staff on hand, they could do a lot of things for her, like telling the other members of staff what to do. Kay was in and out of her office all day nearly. That's where I think the deputy staff would be useful. Also, I think Kay would like to improve things but just hasn't got the time. I think that if they all got together and had a good talk about improving things, it might bring a few smiles to both the clients and the staff. Being so busy, like Kay seemed to be, is nothing to laugh about.

I'm just saying what I feel. I don't know really whether the clients are happy enough or not. I would have liked to have seen the corridors empty and the workshops full, and everyone doing something, instead of just sitting there all day. I would have thought that the young man I saw there all day could have done with a staff member there to see if he was all right. But nobody went near him.

Ford Lane Centre

Report by Simon Gardner

The building is an old British Airways base. The outside looks really scruffy, and the inside looks like a load of old portacabins all put together. They have an art-room-cum-craft room, plus a housecraft room where they can be taught how to do basic cooking. We had lunch there to-day as well. I didn't think much of the lunch at all.

The atmosphere at Ford Lane centre, in the workshop, was very noisy. It was very hard to hear what Mary had to say to me – if she liked the centre and what was going on at the centre. To me, Mary didn't seem very happy there, really.

Now staff, and the way they talked to me, and the way they were in the centre. When I went to get my lunch, the lady behind the hot plate went to give me a dinner which was the same as the other people who attend the centre, but another person came up to her and said 'Oh, the people who have come to-day to look at the centre, their dinner is in the hot plate'. My dinner was being kept specially hot for me. I didn't like that because I felt I was getting special treatment. When I was eating my dinner, the member of staff came over with my sweet and pushed it towards me. I didn't like that.

There were some members of staff who were very, very nice. They asked me questions about what I was doing there, and why I was involved in the evaluation for Hillingdon.

I enjoyed going to the self advocacy meeting in the afternoon, just to see how people communicated with each other. The meeting was run by staff. One of the clients opened the meeting, but a member of staff took over later on. One young lady who was a service user was the chairperson, but I didn't think much of the way she was doing it.

Recommendations

Ford Lane should have more money spent on it so that peoples' lives can be improved. One area where money should be spent is on the building itself, for example, the ramp in the corridor needs attention – it was roughed up which makes it hard to walk on and difficult for people in wheelchairs. The centre was too small and claustrophobic, there was not enough space to swing a cat around. The corridors were too narrow. The outside looked really scruffy.

I don't really think that centres are a very good idea. They are often a waste of time. People often don't learn very much there – they just copy bad habits from other people. I think this is particularly true of this one. Because the centre is so small, there is not much for them to do, and they can become bored.

Greenbank Day Services

Report by Joyce Kershaw

When we arrived we were greeted by a client in a wheelchair who asked if he could help us: he asked us to put our names in the book. We asked to see the Manager. Then one of the staff took us into a big workshop where Paul and John were working. I sat with Paul at a table where he and five other clients were making plastic files. I joined in and helped to do some of these plastic files. Although I knew what to do just by watching them, I let Paul and one or two of the others show me what to do. It makes them feel important and good in themselves. Then John showed us what he was doing and we watched him, and some others cleaning small yellow plastic wheels.

Then we had a talk to a member of staff in the workshop to find out more information. She told us the plastic files were boxed and they were sold in shops. But the yellow plastic rings that John was cleaning were not sent out to be sold. It was just something to do in that workshop. I wouldn't have liked the job – the yellow rings that John and some of the others were cleaning. I'd have asked for something else more important but they thought it important, and that is all that matters for them: to think they are doing something important.

I noticed although we were walking around it did not stop the clients from doing their jobs. It was a nice feeling, I can't really explain what I felt, but wherever I went in the centre the clients made us feel really welcome.

Then Paul and John took us for a tea break in the dining-room, it was large but only a very small kitchen. I thought they could have done with a much larger kitchen.

We did not know really if we should ask Paul and John about their relationships: in other words, if they had a lady friend. But we did not have to because they went and sat on different tables next to their girl friends. They introduced us to their best friends as well. There were a few I saw with their arms round their girl friends.

Then after the break we went into another room where there was a computer. Paul sat down and had a go on it, the staff sat and helped them if they got stuck. It was to teach them how to count and how to tell one colour from the other. There was a young girl in the room and she kept on trying to help the other clients if they got it wrong: but she could not talk properly. I thought it was a shame because she knew but couldn't tell them. She really wanted to help.

There was also a young man who was strapped in a wheelchair. I was thinking how cheerful and handsome he was. I was thinking it is such a shame to be that way. When I see anyone disabled like that, I feel for them.

After dinner we interviewed John in a different room to where he was working. John answered all our questions.

In recreation time for the clients, Andrea, Simon and myself went to interview the Manager. We found him very helpful. We asked him a lot of questions. I asked him if he had already made any changes, or if the clients had asked for anything? He said yes. He told us he got on well with the clients, but now he is a manager, he does not get as much time as he would like to with the clients.

We asked him how he got on with the staff, and he said he liked all the staff, but they did not always agree with what he says or wants for the day centre.

We also asked him if the clients attended any of the staff meetings, and he said they didn't. I think it is important to have the clients' point of view as well as the staff's. We also put to him who did he involve in planning things for the clients and he said their key workers, because a key worker is with them and so they tend to tell the key worker more than the Manager. When we asked him if any of the clients had a job outside, he said yes, so we asked him how many. He told us five in the last six months and ten in the year just gone.

It was a change to see such a young manager for once.

When we had finished he walked with us to show us where to find Paul, and while we were talking he told us about the paint on the walls – the clients had picked the colours. He said some wanted one colour and others wanted another colour, so he had satisfied them all by having the two colours.

Then Simon and myself went home with Paul and John on the mini bus.

It was fun, I enjoyed it very much, because both the clients and the staff were talking to us.

Greenbank Day Services

Report by Simon Gardner

The first thing I did, was go with John into an art class. We went into the room where they did arts and crafts, and so on, and John was drawing some flowers for an Easter card for some relation, and I sat down talking to the tutor or member of staff who was there. She asked me a few questions about what I was doing and I told her why I was there, and she sounded very interested.

The next thing I did was go into the workshop with John and we sat down and were talking about what sort of things he did at the centre – things he liked, things he didn't like. John was wiping little wheels that were used for spools for films. We sat down and were brushing these things off and having a conversation while we were doing it, and talking to some of the other clients in the workshop, on our table. Just talking about things in general, really. It was a good feeling – talking. People kept on pointing at me and saying things like: 'What's he doing here?' Some of them kept asking questions, which I didn't mind answering.

I thought the building was very huge and it took some time to get used to finding my way around. Once I had sussed that out I was O.K. Met some people that I met at the 1988 People First conference, which was great to meet them after a long time. We did an interview with the manager, Joyce and I, which went really great. We talked about the staff in the interview with the manager, which went down O.K. That was the first interview at the centre. Then we interviewed John, which went down very well; it was easy. We asked him questions about what he thought of the centre: do you like coming here; the sort of things he did. He spoke freely and openly to us about what he thought. One or two things with the questions he had problems to answer, so we had to explain them in a different way.

* * *

Services to people from minority groups

People First has always been concerned that the needs of people from minority groups should be properly considered when providing services. They felt it was important to include questions about this in the evaluation.

Although none of the people in the houses came from minority groups, we felt it was important to try and get an idea of what contacts people had with people from other races, cultures and creeds, what the attitudes of staff were to this, and what steps services were taking to make sure that people from minority groups were not forgotten.

People who live in the houses were asked: 'Do you meet with people from other religions and cultures?' None of the residents had any close contact with people from other cultures or minority groups. There were no neighbours from minority groups at Prince Street. At Valley Road, a chinese family who were neighbours was mentioned. One resident mentioned meeting people from other races at work.

Questions to staff were: 'How many people from minority groups are employed by your services?'; and 'Do you have people from minority groups at the centre/hostel?'

There were very few clients or staff from minority groups at the places we visited. One manager said: 'If we had people from ethnic minorities I would want appropriate staff to support them'. Another manager with seven staff from minority groups said that what came first for her was that the person should have the right qualities for the job. She felt that Hillingdon needs a black workers' support group.

A senior manager told us that less than 5 per cent of people employed by social services belong to minority groups. The percentage for the whole population is 10 per cent. Their Equal Opportunities group was looking into the reasons for this.

Getting documents about Hillingdon's plans

Before the evaluation started we were given copies of Hillingdon's Personal Action Plans documents and instructions to staff on how to use it, and copies of their Complaints Procedure, instructions to staff and a leaflet about it for clients.

During the interviews we asked senior staff if they could give us copies of written plans for their services or aims and objectives for their particular part of the service, but they were unable to provide any. It seemed that none existed or copies were not easily obtained: 'No, there isn't anything specific' – 'I think there is something somewhere but I'm not sure where it is', were two of the comments.

Personal Action Plans were not mentioned by any of the residents. They were mentioned in some way, by all staff interviewed. We saw individual records being completed during one of the sessions we sat in on at Greenbank day centre.

Job Shop

We were pleased to take advantage of an unexpected opportunity to visit Hillingdon's Job Shop.

Job Shop is for people with learning difficulties who want full or part-time employment or work experience placements. It offers support with all aspects of getting a job – choosing a suitable job, interview technique, application forms, advice on benefits, and training and support once work starts. It aims to make full use of each person's skills and to find a job which matches those skills.

Employment opportunities mostly come from the voluntary and semi-voluntary sector. Some of the work is done free – £2.50 an hour is charged to those who can afford to pay.

People who seek work through Job Shop fall into three groups:

- ▲ those who are just starting out and are therefore likely to be wanting work experience placements;
- ▲ those who have learnt some skills – they might sometimes do voluntary work and sometimes do work involving a small payment;
- ▲ those who always get paid for the work they do (ten people at the time of our visit).

A wide variety of work is undertaken – e.g. clerical jobs, working with children in creches and playgroups, catering, library work, charity shops, old people's homes. At the time of our visit, Job Shop was inundated with horticultural jobs – fences, gardens, greenhouses etc. – because of damage caused by a recent storm. Some people work in the Job Shop office first before moving on to a work experience placement or other job outside.

Job Shop is able to offer training within its own office. We saw a number of computers, typewriters and other equipment available for people to learn and practise using. It was good to see that Job Shop recognises the importance of people learning general work skills – timekeeping, work social skills, etc. For example, the following 'Ground Rules for Users' were displayed clearly:

GROUND RULES FOR USERS

On arrival, to announce themselves to office.

Coats and bags hung on hooks provided.

No smoking.

No food (except with prior arrangement for project workers).

Wash up.

Punctuality.

Independence (no supervision).

Appropriate attitude to work.

Adhere to coffee, lunch and tea breaks
10.45–11.00 coffee/tea
12.15– 1.15 lunch
2.45– 3.00 coffee/tea

Office Practice Room must be left tidy

Scrap paper must be used for typing practice

Work must be named, dated and filed.

Job Shop is staffed by two full-time workers employed by social services. Overall responsibility is in the hands of the Deputy Manager of one of the day centres. Job Shop has strong links with VOX – Hillingdon's 'high street' employment agency for people with all types of disabilities. They co-operate in searching for suitable jobs and supporting people in their jobs.

We enjoyed our visit to Job Shop and feel it is a very valuable part of the services Hillingdon offers.

5 Recommendations

Services in Hillingdon should:

- ▲ Make sure the houses they buy for people are close to shops and public transport – not only so that the people who live there can learn to use the shops and buses, but to make it easy for people to visit them.
- ▲ Think very carefully about how they choose people to live in the houses – particularly how people communicate with each other – so that none of them will feel left out. For example, a person with a severe hearing disability with other people who can't do sign language.
- ▲ Do more to help people look after their own money and medication, so that they will feel more independent.
- ▲ Enable people to have locks on their bedroom doors and bathroom doors to make sure people can have privacy. It is possible to do this and still be able to get in in an emergency.
- ▲ Make sure that people understand the Complaints Procedure. It is important to know what to do if you can't get a problem solved easily.
- ▲ Help staff to work out good ways of making sure the residents meet people who might become friends – especially people who are not connected with services.
- ▲ Provide more opportunities for people to do different things in the daytime. More staff are needed to help people learn real skills.
- ▲ Give staff more training on how to help people who have been in institutions for a long time.
- ▲ Enable staff to spend more time on travel training and helping people to use public transport.
- ▲ Provide more opportunities for staff to help people who have difficulty communicating – more courses to learn signing; more help from speech therapists over a longer period of time.
- ▲ Provide resources to enable ordinary citizens to become advocates of the residents. One way of doing this would be to set up a citizen advocacy scheme.

In conclusion

We think that the services have done very well in helping the residents in their own homes. The residents have learnt a lot of new skills, and can do a lot more for themselves. They are more confident and independent. They feel good in themselves and are happy in the houses.

With regard to what they do in the daytime and in their leisure time, services have made some good progress with some individual people but there is a lot still to be done.

When it comes to helping people make friends and be really involved in their local community, services are still 'at the starting gate'.

There are a lot of enthusiastic staff in Hillingdon who want to help people have better lives. This includes senior staff as well as those who work in the houses. Senior staff must support staff in the houses, so that they can carry out the good ideas and plans they have for the people who live there.

We hope that anyone looking at these two houses in a year's time will be able to say that services have made a lot of progress in helping the people who live there enjoy life with lots of friends, choices and opportunities.

6 How the evaluation team felt about the work

Simon Gardner

I enjoyed it. It was a challenge. I'd never done this sort of thing before. I learned a lot about myself – my strengths and weaknesses – got to know myself a bit better from it.

What I will remember is the atmosphere in Prince Street – welcoming you like you were part of the family. That will always stick in my mind – always!

I found it difficult to talk to the women at Valley Road because of the age group. Communicating with two of the people in Prince Street was the hardest part. I wish I was able to communicate better with both of them than I did. I felt out of it, not being able to communicate.

I found it a bit of a strain sometimes, rushing here and there. I feel I learnt to cope with the rushing round in a very short space of time. I didn't think I would be able to cope with it because of not being able to sleep sometimes, but I did. It gave me a big boost doing the evaluation.

Joyce Kershaw

When Andrea asked me if I would like to do this interviewing, she said it'll be hard, and so it has been, not just for me but the three of us. Although it's been hard and tiring sometimes, I've enjoyed it. I'd do it all over again if I was asked.

I think what makes it so difficult is trying to get the men and women in the two houses to understand you, and it was very hard for us to understand them too.

Simon and myself had one or two disagreements, but I suppose that's what it's all about – it wouldn't do if we agreed on everything.

I know at some of the things I've seen I was shocked. I only hope after all we have done, some good will come out of it. That would really make me feel happy.

I really felt smashing and important. I know one thing, I wouldn't have missed it for anything.

Andrea Whittaker

Like the consultants, I really enjoyed the work and felt privileged to be a part of it. It was good to be involved in such a new and important opportunity for people with learning difficulties.

Perhaps the most challenging feature of the work for me was the need to support the consultants properly without contributing my own ideas or opinions. In most circumstances, working as a team with colleagues, you discuss each phase of the work, share opinions, debate causes etc. This situation was quite different – it was important to work in a way which ensured as far as possible that I did not influence the consultants. To be a part of the evaluation team and yet not be able to share my enthusiasm – and sometimes my dismay – about what we saw, was quite a discipline!

With regard to practical ways of helping without influencing, I concentrated on the process rather than the content. For example, Simon and Joyce were mostly very good at asking supplementary questions during the course of an interview, but occasionally there were times when I felt that more probing might be appropriate. My contribution then was to suggest that they might ask some further questions, rather than saying what those questions might be.

At times, I found myself feeling anxious about the issue of making a balanced or 'fair' judgement. Mostly I refrained from commenting, taking the view that this evaluation was not about looking at all sides of a question but about learning what users of services see and feel, based on their own life experience. However, occasionally I suggested that the consultants consider whether there might be other ways of looking at an issue, or other reasons why a situation might be as it is – without stating what I thought the other ways or reasons might be. Sometimes this led to further thinking on an issue, sometimes it didn't.

I learnt a lot about planning a project of this nature and the time it takes to do. I was very conscious of the pressure to complete the work by the Regional conference day (13 July).

Being responsible for the organising and administration, as well as providing the transport and accommodation, sometimes felt a bit much for one person, but on the whole it worked well.

7 What worked well and what could have been better

The points are first listed as a summary and then some of them are discussed in more detail.

Worked well

- ▲ WE WORKED WELL TOGETHER AS A TEAM
- ▲ RECORDING THE INFORMATION
- ▲ HELPING PEOPLE UNDERSTAND THE QUESTIONS
- ▲ PRACTICAL ORGANISATION
  - – SUPPORT AT KING'S FUND CENTRE
  - – SUPPORT AT HILLINGDON
- ▲ WE ALL ENJOYED IT!

Could have been better

- ▲ PARTS OF QUESTIONNAIRES
  - – DIFFICULT QUESTIONS
  - – ABSTRACT QUESTIONS
- ▲ WE NEEDED MORE TIME TO GET TO KNOW PEOPLE IN THE HOUSES BEFORE WE INTERVIEWED THEM.
- ▲ MORE PREPARATION TIME NEEDED, e.g. to draw up QUESTIONNAIRES to work out DIFFERENT WAYS OF INTERVIEWING
- ▲ NUMBER OF INTERVIEWS WITH FAMILY MEMBERS
- ▲ TRAVELLING
  - – DRIVING
  - – NOT KNOWING THE AREA

Recording the information

Joyce filled in the questionnaires as the interviews proceeded, and also wrote additional notes at other times.

Andrea also completed the questionnaires.

Simon used a dictaphone to record thoughts and opinions.

This system worked well.

Helping people understand the questions

Joyce and Simon were good at asking questions in different ways, thinking of examples to explain a question, sometimes acting out an example to help understanding. This worked well with most of the people but it did not overcome the communication difficulties with two of the residents in particular. One young man with severe hearing disability relies on sign language to communicate beyond the superficial level. Another 26-year-old man is just beginning to learn letters, words and numbers, using picture cards, and his spoken vocabulary is still very limited. Simon recorded his experience of interviewing this young man:

> *I felt physically and mentally drained from this interview, because I haven't got the skills to sign in Makaton. I had to make the questions a little bit simpler so that I could make Paul understand what I was trying to ask him. I had to show him one thing – it was about privacy – like if someone was in the bathroom, having a bath or was on the loo, about knocking on the door and a resident was in there. I think he understood that question after I had physically showed him what I meant, rather than explaining it to him.*
>
> *Half way through the interview, Joyce took over because I was beginning to feel shattered and Joyce finished the interview. When she had finished, she looked shattered as well.*

The information we had before we began the evaluation did not prepare us for the severity of these communication problems. Although we made attempts to secure aids such as picture sets, there was not enough time to find these – or develop our own – or work out any new ways of communicating with people in this type of situation.

With hindsight, we needed more time between our first meeting with the residents and when the interviewing started, in order to select the most effective way of interviewing these people.

The questionnaires

The majority of the questions worked well for us. This was because:

- ▲ they were questions that People First members wanted to ask;
- ▲ they were phrased in the words of People First members.

However, we learnt a lot about which questions did not work so well. Some were too difficult for the people we interviewed to answer. They needed to be asked using different words. We couldn't always think of the right 'different words' quickly. Some questions were too abstract for people to understand. We needed to use different ways of 'interviewing' them to get the information. We didn't have enough time to work on this before the interviewing started.

Questionnaire layout

This worked well. It was clearly laid out and easy to read. We left plenty of white space! We also put a dark line across the page under each question to help make it easy to see the questions.

Backup support

At the King's Fund Centre. Good, speedy, computerised secretarial backup helped a great deal, particularly during the very concentrated two weeks of interviewing.
At Hillingdon. It was good to be allocated our own office at Laurel Lodge for working in between interviews. The staff there were also very helpful.

The timetable

It would have been better to have allowed more time to prepare for the work – to develop the questionnaires and learn more about interviewing.

There should have been a longer gap between when we first met the residents and when the interviews started. We would have then had more chance to seek advice and work out the best ways of interviewing people, particularly those who used signing to communicate. In order to get to know one of the residents in particular, we would have had to spend a lot more time than was available in this evaluation.

The actual two weeks for doing the visits and interviews worked well on the whole. Drawing up the timetable, which in the end involved 19 interviews and ten visits, was complicated but not impossible! We must say, here, that it certainly couldn't have been done without the willing cooperation of the staff and residents of both houses!

It was tiring doing two weeks' concentrated work, but we felt it was better to do it that way than separate the two weeks. This might have meant having to re-learn things and refresh our memories before starting the second week.

Interviews with family members

It was disappointing that we were only able to interview two of the residents' relatives. As explained earlier, we felt that the people at Valley Road didn't really want us to talk to their relatives and we respected their wishes. We met the mother of one of the men at Prince Street and the grandmother of another. We were unable to interview relatives of the other two men because of personal circumstances in the families at the time of our visit.

Travelling

We couldn't have done the work without a car. A lot of driving was involved. It was quite difficult at the beginning of the two 'interviewing' weeks, not knowing the area. It took the first three or four days for Andrea, our driver/navigator, to be reasonably familiar with the various routes we had to negotiate. This felt quite time-consuming though it only seriously interfered with the timetable once when we got lost one evening and had to abandon plans to go to one of the clubs. We also had to drive from Finchley to Hillingdon and back each day. For a future occasion we would recommend that the consultants should be able to stay in the area where the evaluation is taking place.

PART II

WHAT WE LEARNT

8 An independent view of the evaluation

An independent report of People First's work by Libby Cooper, Director, Charities Evaluation Services.

Introduction

My role

My role as evaluator was essentially one of an observer – to offer advice on the process of carrying out the study rather than the content of the research itself. The latter was determined by People First.

My involvement as evaluator of the evaluation included:

(i) two preliminary meetings with the consultants and supporter to discuss research methods;
(ii) observation of the two consultants over a period of two days (one in each house) whilst they interviewed residents;
(iii) two further meetings with the evaluation team to discuss analysis of the data;
(iv) an interview with each consultant;
(v) a meeting with the Supporter to discuss the draft report.

I provided the research team with guidelines on the best means of recording information so that data could be related to specific individuals, suggested a re-ordering of topics and insisted that some attempt should be made to compare residents' previous situations with the present. The latter was perhaps my only intrusive input, since it was vital to maintain the principle of 'control' by People First. I also discussed issues concerned with interviewing.

The early period in the development of the research was exciting and the ways in which the interview-questionnaires were developed were impressive.

Clearly, from my initial observations I felt that the team worked well together. The skills of the consultants tended to complement each other and the supporter was superb in handling the situation in a purely supportive rather than advisory role.

Evaluation

In evaluating the final evaluation, three sets of criteria can be used:

Firstly, and most importantly, it should be evaluated on its own terms, that is in terms of the objectives set down by NW Thames Regional Health Authority and Hillingdon Social Services, as well as those declared by People First.

Secondly, it can be evaluated against alternative approaches.

Thirdly, it can be evaluated against the standards of research methodology.

1. Evaluation in terms of original objectives

This evaluation – the first of its kind for people with learning difficulties – is an important new approach and it is, therefore, most relevant to evaluate it in its own terms.

The Regional Health Authority's objective is:

▲ to involve consumers in service delivery by looking at down-to-earth services from the view-point of users.

People First's objective is:

▲ to help its members stand up for themselves and take more control over their lives.

Thus People First saw the opportunity of working for the Region as a means of reaching this objective. An important outcome in the long term for them, therefore, is to obtain the feeling that others are taking notice of what they are saying. They would be disappointed to find that their report had been left on a shelf like so many academic reports; instead they wish to be involved in implementing its results.

An important part of the value-system in the work of People First is that their members can relate to people with learning difficulties more easily than staff or professional researchers because they have relevant personal experience.

Some evaluations suffer from discordant values but there is clearly a commendable merging of values here between those of the region and those of People First.

Expected outputs

A number of expectations can be predicted from this way of working:

a) Evaluation outputs

– A good clear report providing a set of recommendations focusing on the real needs of residents, which can be implemented within available resources;

– A report which is sympathetic to those needs;

– A piece of work which has been carried out well.

b) Process outputs

– Evaluation which has been conducted in a less threatening manner;

– Evaluation which has been participative.

c) Short-term and long-term outcomes

– Greater impact on policy makers because of the way it has been conducted;

– Increased self confidence of those who completed the work and an impact on the development of People First as a group;

– More involvement at the policy making level by consumers.

a) Evaluation outputs

The final product, I believe, has provided a very clear picture for the providers of services to people with learning difficulties. The Region has clearly achieved its aim of successfully moving the residents into community houses. Essentially, however, the evaluation has found that there is a clear disparity between satisfaction with new residential care and an involvement in the community. Findings are that residents have been given more choice in their living standards and have increased in competence. As yet, the same cannot be said for the ways in which they live their lives outside of the house. This is an important finding and one which can now be tackled by management.

The focus of the research has been very direct and sympathetic in that its results emerge from an understanding of the perceptions of residents themselves.

Thus I can say that the objective of ascertaining the needs of residents as perceived by them has been reached.

b) Process outputs

Regarding the process of carrying out the research, it has, indeed, been conducted in a very participative manner which is less threatening to residents than perhaps a study by professional researchers who sometimes assume a relationship of authority. There is no doubt that residents in institutions have experienced many situations where they have felt they are the subject of study rather than a participant. Researchers, too, have theorised about their relationship with those they interview but from my observation I felt the relationship between researcher and 'the researched' in this study was extremely good.

An interview period of two weeks, where the consultants not only conducted interviews in the houses but also visited day centres and leisure activities, was very appropriate in helping overcome this problem. It allowed relationships to be formed between consultants and residents and broke down the kind of barriers which might otherwise be present.

The major weakness in this approach, however, as already identified in the report, was the fact that there was no time between initial meetings in the houses and the beginning of the interview sessions. As mentioned previously, some residents had severe communication difficulties and the research team could have accommodated to that fact, given more time. I would, therefore, recommend that future studies ensure a two week preparation period at this time to take account of the individual needs of residents. During this time it would be useful to adapt some of the interview topics into visual representation – pictures of houses, furniture, leisure facilities, people communicating etc.

My observation of the consultants at work showed that they had great insight into the problems experienced by residents. Their manner was also respectful, tactful and friendly so that an easy atmosphere was created. Both consultants developed skilful methods of interviewing, although as a professional researcher I sometimes felt that I would like to have picked up on some issues and delved further into them. They were also creative in asking questions in different ways when residents had difficulty in understanding. The areas investigated by the consultants also seemed very relevant to the everyday life of residents.

On the whole, I felt that the information gathered from residents was very reliable but the major weakness in the research was the lack of data from other sources which could be used for supplementing and verifying their comments. Further discussion of research methodology follows below.

c) Short-term and long-term outcomes

Concerning the issue of increased confidence of the consultants, my observation and interviews with them demonstrated that they had gained an enormous amount of self esteem.

> *'I felt excited and proud that I had been asked . . . I looked forward to going back and seeing all those faces again . . . I felt I could not let them down . . . I felt important asking all those questions'.*

The main reason why they considered they were particularly appropriate for carrying out the work was because they felt their personal experiences had given them the ability to identify with and understand the lives of the residents. It is not surprising to find, therefore, that their major fears were that they might not be accepted by the residents in the houses. Here we can see that the main value of People First comes to the fore. At the end of the study the consultants felt they had been successful in achieving this identification with the residents.

Research is a task incorporating many different skills and it is often helpful if more than one researcher works on a study. Interviews with the consultants revealed that their skills were complementary. One of them found interviewing more difficult and tiring, whilst the process of analysing the data came easier to one than the other. Both were unanimous in their respect for the supporter's help and felt that they would like more training in the future.

Clearly, the process outcomes of the research have been of the highest order – from the early meetings between People First and the supporter, to the development of techniques, the conducting of interviews and the analysis of data. It is perhaps at the analytic stage that I was able to perceive the greatest increase in confidence. The two consultants had gained more knowledge not only of the needs of residents but also of the whole process of research and became clearer in what they saw as outcomes.

Assessing long term outcomes is, of course, more difficult. My observation of the meeting between the evaluation team, members of the regional health authority and Hillingdon social services, when the evaluation results were first discussed, revealed that managers were indeed interested in the results. They were ready to hear criticism. The fact that a conference was funded by the region in order that their employees and managers could learn from the exercise suggests that consumers voices may be more clearly heard. Whether this results in actually influencing policy makers is yet to be determined.

In terms of the original objectives and implicit values, then, the research has been very successful. The region has a report which can now be used for action. If they can implement these recommendations and involve other members of People First in the development of their policies concerning community care, the long term outcomes of the research will have been reached.

My final point, however, refers to what I consider to be the major weakness in the evaluation. It is not a weakness in terms of the original objectives laid down by the commissioners of the evaluation. The fact that People First have been involved in this very important study is very commendable but it is not to be confused with true empowerment. The focus of the evaluation has been purely on the needs of residents as perceived by themselves. This approach leaves the institutional framework untouched.

Although some interviews were conducted with staff in the houses, the issues were perhaps a little too schematic and unrelated to organisational management to be of greater benefit in the longer term. For instance, at the simple level the comment made by one member of staff about 'problems with red tape' is an issue that should have been investigated in greater depth. Nor have issues of staff development and training been drawn out. Social workers, organisational managers and policy makers have not been sufficiently incorporated in the evaluation.

2. Evaluation in terms of alternative approaches

Two research studies will be used.

Evaluation of residental homes for elderly people

The first concerns an evaluation carried out by elderly volunteers who stayed in residential homes for elderly people for a period of one week.[7] During this time they wrote up a diary of their experiences and impressions and offered detailed opinions on the quality and appropriateness of the care offered. There are clearly similarities between their study and that of People First.

One of the difficulties in their method of evaluation concerns the fact that there was no real framework created at the beginning of the research to ensure that all volunteers focused on the same issues. As discussed below this is an important feature of research methodology. Also since each volunteer only stayed in one home there was no means of comparing results. A further dilemma was posed by the fact that the volunteers could not put themselves into the position of residents and were often defended against doing so in an attempt to retain their future independence.

However, one of the findings by the research consultant who analysed the results suggests that 'the speed with which the volunteers took on the ethos of the institutions, the haste with which they were willing to conform and the difficulties they perceived of asserting their own preferences, emphasise that formal consultation with a small group of 'representative' residents, important though it is, will not in itself provide sufficient means of offering choice to every individual resident'.

This is an issue to be thought through by all policy makers in their desire to include consumers in their evaluation. This present evaluation does not suffer from the same problem, since the consultants, although they have previously experienced institutional care, are now in a position of independence and can therefore be more demanding.

Finally, in terms of recommendations, the study of elderly people's homes is consequently luke warm in its findings and reticent in criticism. The People First evaluation is superior and has a clearer analysis of results from their study.

National study of community care changes

The second study concerns one of the most important evaluations of community care conducted by The Care in the Community Team at The Personal Social Services Research Unit at Kent University.[8] Their study lasted four years and therefore there can be no direct comparison with People First's evaluation, but in looking at some of their methodology we can perhaps see some elements which are lacking from the People First's study.

The PSSRU's major foci were 'client outcomes, organisational processes, staffing logistics, changes in psycho-social and physical environments and costs and resources'. Nineteen key questions structured the evaluation and frameworks were devised for each of them. A huge set of data was generated from this research, with complex sets of inter-relationships and a wide range of perspectives at the project and client levels. Since the research was commissioned by the DHSS it is likely to have a considerable impact on the development of policy at government level.

The PSSRU's research which related to nearly 800 people who had been moved into the community suggests that fears held by some people that community care policies might result in former residents being more vulnerable to exploitation, destitution or delinquency are unfounded.

But what is of most relevance to my evaluation is their findings in relation to outcomes for people with learning difficulties. The community care programme promoted significant improvements in their quality of life but incured marginally higher community care costs. Integration proved to be more of a problem for this particular client group, education and employment being common areas of difficulty. Social contacts were lower in the community than in hospital, but clients expressed significantly greater levels of satisfaction with their social contacts. Marked improvements in clients' skill levels were found especially in 'ordinary living' situations.

Like our study it was not always possible to interview all clients to assess morale and life satisfaction but the evidence from those able to communicate indicates higher levels of satisfaction with community living when compared with life in hospital.

These findings are surprisingly close to those found in the People First study and the consultants should be commended for their hard work. Thus in evaluating like with like – that is a focus on client outcome – there are great similarities in the results, even though the PSSRU study would clearly be more detailed following a four year study.

It is presumably at the organisational level of community initiatives and the allocation of resources that the PSSRU research can influence policy makers. This is an area which should be incorporated in future user-led evaluation studies.

3. Evaluation in terms of research methodology

Generally speaking there are seven stages of conducting evaluation:

(i) *preparation* – which involves questioning why the evaluation is to be conducted and for whom it will be carried out.

(ii) *design* – which involves agreeing what is to be evaluated, aims of the evaluation and the agreement of criteria against which the scheme will be evaluated. Key issues to be addressed are determined at this stage to provide an evaluative framework, as are appropriate methods of data collection and means of recording that information. It is also important at this stage to have a clear idea of how the generated information will be analysed and fed back.

(iii) *data collection* – this involves collecting information and recording it in a form which can be used by the evaluators.

(iv) *interpretation* – refers to the stage at which the data is ordered and analysed in terms of the original framework of investigation. Comparisons are then made between sets of data.

(v) *assessment* – which is made from the analysis of the data as to the value of the work under scrutiny and presented in a useful form together with recommendations for change.

(vi) *implementation* – information from the evaluation study is fed back into the organisation to inform policy direction, change working methods or improve upon service delivery, etc. This is a process which can be carried out throughout the evaluation to inform further stages of work, depending upon the way in which the evaluation has been designed.

(vii) *review* – an organisation benefits mostly when evaluation becomes a normal part of its work. Therefore, following the implementation of a first study, it is important to review the evaluation process which has been conducted and to ensure that ongoing forms of monitoring and evaluation are incorporated in the work practice of the organisation.

In reality this process is rarely so clear-cut. A number of these elements overlap and some stages take far longer than others, particularly the design stage.

For a variety of reasons in recent years there has been a move from experimental, cross-sectional or cost-effectiveness studies towards what is often termed 'pluralistic evaluation'. This method accepts that many understandings of aims, objectives, success and failure exist amongst all those people involved in an organisation and that it is inappropriate to assume that the meeting of one single criterion is sufficient evidence of achievement. Thus a variety of qualitative and quantitative methods are used to reveal the differing interpretations of how programmes have met the needs of local people and whether resources have been used most effectively.

In the case of People First's evaluation there was a clear brief which determined what was to be evaluated, i.e. client satisfaction with their new living conditions. Clearly, interviews with residents was the most relevant research method for their study. But the major weakness in the research was that very little data was gathered from other sources which could confirm residents' comments. The evaluation team have already acknowledged that they were unsuccessful in talking to relatives.

If we focus on one of the major issues for all researchers when they are looking at the needs of others – we can see that there is always a problem in creating a balance between realising that we all find it difficult to articulate what we really need yet would not wish others to take the initiative for us. Clients in institutional settings unfortunately have been more used to the latter than the former and an evaluation such as this offers them the opportunity to voice their rights, perhaps for the first time. However, if we take as a starting point that residents have been institutionalised for many years (a finding in this evaluation which has implications for creating more community involvement) then it is even more difficult to demonstrate that there are other ways of living.

Therefore, by adopting a 'pluralistic' methodology several issues can be investigated from different perspectives which allows more insight into new possibilities for change. For instance, if interviews and observations of other clients were also conducted in the original residential homes there would have been more comparative data for consultants to use when determining whether real changes had taken place in the lives of residents. If more interviews had been conducted with senior management, then issues concerning effective allocation of resources, staff development and efficiency could have been investigated as well as their understandings of the benefits of community care policies.

A further weakness in the research concerns the fact that a framework for analysis was not determined at the beginning of the design period but following data collection. In the event, the matrix incorporating O'Brien's Five Accomplishments[5] proved to be an extremely useful tool in helping the consultants make sense of all the data they had collected. In future studies, however, it would be recommended that such a matrix is looked at carefully during the design phase to determine indicators of outcome for each accomplishment and then to match these with the contents of the interview-questionnaires.

Concerning the contents of the questionnaires themselves, generally speaking they worked well, particularly those for residents. These have been discussed and will be changed in accordance with the weaknesses identified by the evaluation team and myself.

The main problems with the questionnaires were that some questions were too abstract for residents and occasionally probes were too difficult for the interviewers to deal with. On some occasions it would have been beneficial to acquire more concrete examples – for instance, on how staff actually help residents, in what ways residents are treated with respect, how their increased confidence was demonstrated, how many visitors arrive at the houses.

The Living With Other People and the Leisure questionnaires worked well, perhaps because they came directly from the experiences of the consultants. The day centre questionnaire, however, could have been developed further with more questions concerning organisational and management issues.

The weakest questionnaires were those addressed to staff and centre managers. Bearing in mind that staff were in a position to give more in-depth information about themselves, residents and management, I felt a good opportunity had been missed.

The questionnaire for family was also too short and could have been developed further.

In terms of evaluating the research against the principles of 'good' research methodology, I think I have highlighted weak areas. However, the results are no less reliable or invalid because of these failings. Indeed, the additional benefits identified above far outweigh the costs. We are involved in community research here – what we might call 'bottom-up research' rather than 'top-down research'. The consultants have been supremely successful in achieving that aim.

Recommendations

1. More time should be given to evaluators to assess the communication levels of residents before they are interviewed.

2. Unpatronising pictures should be devised for residents with communication problems.

3. A more pluralistic approach should be adopted.

4. All interviews and questionnaires should be developed in accordance with the matrix incorporating O'Brien's key accomplishments.

5. Questionnaires for senior managers should be developed.

6. People First should be involved in policy making discussions at a more senior level.

7. All researchers need help with one area or another of their work, thus a collaborative approach should be adopted whereby people with learning difficulties are given research support and training in interviewing, in such a way that they remain in control of the evaluation process and are not turned into 'professionals'.

9 Key elements for success in a service-user led evaluation

All three members of the evaluation team learnt a lot from doing this work. What follows is a summary of what we feel are the most important points to consider in undertaking similar work.

▲ Commitment from service managers

Securing commitment from people at all levels in the service to be evaluated is the vital first stage in any work of this nature. Words are not enough. They must be backed up with resources, support, and a commitment to take action on the findings.

This evaluation would not have happened without the commitment and enthusiasm of key senior managers in Hillingdon Social Services Department and NW Thames RHA. These people were prepared not only to work together across service boundaries to reach agreement in principle to such a new undertaking, but to back this up with appropriate financial and other resources – for example, fees, expenses, office accommodation.

▲ Commitment from 'grassroots' staff

The fact that Hillingdon had a well-established policy of involving service users, demonstrated in practice, meant that staff supporting people in their day-to-day lives welcomed this initiative and were ready and willing to co-operate with the evaluators.

▲ Involve service users right from the start

It is crucial to involve people with learning difficulties at every stage. This is a basic principle underpinning this work, since it is important to make sure that the 'ownership' of the work remains with the service users.

▲ Provide the right support

Personal/advisory support

It is essential that anyone providing support to service users who are involved in evaluations should be experienced in enabling people to express their own views. The supporter needs to work in such a way as to ensure that his or her views do not intrude – that the possibility of him/her influencing the service users is minimised as much as possible. The supporter needs skills in giving 'neutral' advice'. For example, being able to suggest various options for asking questions, leaving the choice of options to the consultants.

Practical support

Transport, meals, accommodation, secretarial back-up, 'office space' – a place that the evaluation team can call their own – for storage, for reviewing progress, for recording impressions and results, for quiet thinking and relaxing!

▲ Allow plenty of preparation time

The amount of preparation time needs to be planned carefully. With hindsight we needed more preparation time, though we became aware also that a balance needs to be struck between allowing enough time to prepare properly and not spending so much time preparing that it spoils the initial enthusiasm and dedication to the work.

Preparation time is needed –

– to devise questionnaires – allowing enough time to prepare first drafts, to get some help from a questionnaire 'expert' and finally to revise them;

– to prepare the consultants and their supporter;

– to get to know the people with learning difficulties you will be interviewing.

This last point was the area where we most needed to allow more time. Although we had a profile of each person (see sample in Part III) – their weekly activities, what they did in the daytime, what they did in the evenings, what they usually did at the week-end – and a certain amount of information about their ability to communicate, this was not sufficient to prepare us for some of the difficulties we encountered with people whose ability to communicate verbally was very limited.

So, you need to allow time to consider carefully what will be the best way of communicating with each person. Would pictures or drawings be helpful? Do you need to take photographs of 'before' and 'after' situations and places? Will you need assistance with interpreting people's answers? For example, someone who is experienced at signing? It would be best if this help is provided by an outside (independent) person. Have you got the money to pay this person?

▲ Training for the consultants

It is likely that people with learning difficulties who are going to be involved in evaluating will already have some of the necessary skills, (e.g. experience at speaking up for themselves, the ability to get on well with people; are interested in other people and what they think and feel). But they will need additional skills particularly relevant when evaluating. They need to learn interviewing skills. They need to work out which method of recording information will suit them best (e.g. writing; using a dictaphone; having someone else write their comments for them.)

▲ Teamwork

It is important that the service user consultants and their supporter work well as a team. Doing this work can be physically and emotionally tiring, and if you don't get on well, it is unlikely you will do a successful piece of work.

10 Issues for the future

This evaluation is an extremely important 'first' because it took the involvement of people with learning difficulties in assessing the quality of services, further than it has ever gone before. Now we need to consider how we can learn from the experience in Hillingdon in order to strengthen this involvement. How does this evaluation fit in with the range of initiatives aimed at achieving and maintaining high quality services which reflect the needs and wishes of people who use those services? Following are a number of questions which we feel need to be explored further in order to develop this work in a positive way.

Involving professionals

One of the important issues for consideration for the future is how much professional expertise should be included. In the case of this evaluation, it is true that more professional involvement at the design stage of the questionnaires, for example, would have resulted in fewer inappropriate questions from a researcher's point of view, but how much of the freshness and enthusiasm of People First ideas might have been lost – or at least 'watered down' – in the process? Perhaps, at least on this pioneering occasion, it was a good thing that the balance of input weighed heavily on People First's side.

Training for consultants

We need to build in time and resources to enable consultants to have relevant training; in interviewing techniques for example – asking supplementary questions, when to keep probing for an answer and when to stop, avoiding leading questions.

On the other hand, we do not want to turn people into quasi-researchers. Given the long history of services casting people with disabilities in a patient/pupil role it would be all too easy to try to turn people into role models which would be acceptable to professionals but which could blunt the uniqueness of their personal contribution.

How do we get the balance right?

Making a balanced judgement

In this work, we are asking for the service users' point of view, but how much can/should we help people to take into account a broader range of views and information before making a judgement? To what extent might the lack of this skill weaken the validity of the judgement? Are there certain areas where this might be important and others where it is less important?

How can we involve users effectively in service evaluation at the senior level as well as grass roots level?

As Libby Cooper points out in her report, the parts of the evaluation which proved most successful in terms of quality of the questionnaires, the interviews and observation, and the judgements made, were those which related to people's everyday lives – home, work, day centre, leisure – and this is perhaps to be expected because it is based on service users' direct experience. The part of the evaluation which from a researcher's point of view was less successful was that involving staff, particularly middle and senior staff.

In developing the questionnaires to staff, People First members had very clear ideas about what they wanted to ask. For example, they were conscious of the need for staff to be properly supported; they wanted to ask questions relating to people from minority groups; they wanted to know how much service users were involved in interviewing and appointing staff. On more than one occasion, their questions took managers by surprise and made them think afresh.

To the extent that the questionnaires to managers and staff were made up of the questions which People First members wanted to ask, they achieved their purpose. The consultants were able to use the information gained to supplement their knowledge of the residents' lives and to help make judgements about the services in general. They gave a service user's view of the staff and management.

Undoubtedly service users have shown that they can contribute to the monitoring and evaluation of services at the management level as well as at 'grassroots' level. For the future, we need to consider how that contribution can be strengthened. Perhaps, in this area it will be made most effective by working alongside professional researchers.

One way forward might be for service user consultants to carry out interviews with senior managers, in partnership with a researcher who has the necessary degree of skill to probe deeply. The roles and boundaries of each would need to be defined. The more experienced interviewer would need to be somebody skilled in working in partnership with the service user in order not to become dominant at the interview.

Another suggestion would be to use small discussion groups – not more than six people – perhaps three with learning difficulties and three senior managers – led by a skilled facilitator. Discussion would take place in the setting to be evaluated, and would be loosely structured around broad areas of living rather than specific questions as in a formal questionnaire.

Keeping 'ownership' with the service users

However we tackle these issues in the future, we must make sure that the support is given in partnership with service users in a way which enhances and does not supplant the unique contribution which they can make because of their own life experience.

This evaluation has shown that people with learning difficulties can take part in the monitoring and evaluation of services in a very direct way. Now there is a base line from which to explore how to develop and strengthen their involvement in such work in the future.

PART III

PRACTICAL GUIDELINES

11 Obtaining users' views

Obtaining users' views

As has been said earlier, we needed more preparation time to get to know the people who lived in the houses in order to work out the best way of communicating with each of them. The methods we used – questionnaires, informal conversation and observation – were not enough in themselves to overcome some residents' severe communication difficulties.

The aim of this section is to give readers an idea of the variety of ways of getting service users' views which have been tried in the past, and point to sources of more detailed information. It is not within our expertise to make a critical assessment of the pros and cons of various methods. In any case, this is done in considerable detail in most of the references we have chosen. We leave it to readers to make up their own minds which method or methods will be the best for their own particular situation.

What follows is a brief summary of some of the methods discussed in the books we have listed. We are particularly indebted to the excellent review of the relevant literature in the book *Outward Bound* by Tim Booth *et al.*, an account of how people with learning difficulties living in Kirklees were helped to move into new homes in the community.

Talking to people

There are a lot of different ways of asking questions:

▲ use of stylised facial drawings – sad to happy faces

▲ straight yes, no, don't know answers

▲ open-ended questions

▲ multiple choice questions

▲ pictorial multiple choice questions.

Using pictures

▲ Taking photographs of typical places/situations in a person's life before and after moving – e.g. old home, new home; old kitchen, new kitchen.

▲ Asking people to draw pictures of themselves which can be used at different stages of an evaluation.

Playing games

For example, the 'posting' game – a way of answering which doesn't involve speaking.[9] Three boxes are used. One labelled with a drawing of the resident's own home, the other two labelled 'good residence', 'bad residence'. Statements are written on individual cards. For example, 'this is a place where people come into your bedroom all the time without knocking'. Residents are asked to put the statement in the appropriate box. A similar process can be used for statements about staff.

The 'Ideal Home' visual game:[10] people are asked to sort cards showing key features of residential settings into three categories; 'Important, Don't know/Don't mind'; 'Unimportant'.

We recommend that readers treat these examples only as a starting point. This is a very interesting area of research, but it is beyond the scope of this publication to go into the various methods and issues in greater detail.

12 The questionnaires

The questionnaires used in the evaluation were devised by People First members. How this is done is described in the report.

This section includes a sample set of all the questionnaires, revised as explained below. We hope they will be useful to people doing similar work. This does not mean, though, that they should be slavishly copied! So, readers *may* like to use the questionnaires as they stand. But you may also decide to alter them to suit your own needs – or devise your own. Interviewing people is a skilled job. Interviewers need to feel comfortable with the words used in the questionnaires. They need training and time to practise the necessary skills.

What is important is that the questionnaires should not be used 'in isolation'. Decisions about their use should be taken in consultation with your local service users and taking into account the other important considerations about doing this work that are described elsewhere in this book.

How the questionnaires were revised

Overall, the questionnaires worked well but as we used them, we discovered where the weaknesses lay. Some questions were too difficult for the person interviewed to understand. Others were too abstract. When compiling the questionnaires we had done our best to avoid leading questions (that is, questions which suggest what the answer might be) and on the whole this was achieved. But some leading questions did slip through! The consultants were able to get round some of these problems by asking extra (supplementary) questions but it is not always easy to think of the right extra questions quickly.

Having discovered which questions did not work well we felt it was wise to try and improve them before printing this publication. We also felt it was important to involve People First members in any revision in order to make sure that the 'ownership' of the ideas remained with People First.

In the event, because of time constraints, we were only partially successful in involving People First members in the revision. Therefore, we have only made changes to the questions in the following instances:

- ▲ those questions which the two consultants themselves found difficult during the evaluation;
- ▲ those questions for which we have genuinely been able to get new ideas from People First members;
- ▲ those questions which our evaluator pointed out as being obvious ones needing change – e.g. 'leading' questions.

This has resulted in approximately 24 questions out of an original total of 156 in the questionnaires being changed.

The following are examples of questions which we have altered.

Original question – 'Is the house what you imagined it to be?' (Too abstract)
New question – 'Did you come to see the house before moving in?'

Original question – 'Do the other people in the house understand about privacy?' (Too difficult/abstract)
New questions – 'Do the other people in the house knock before coming into your room?
Is there a lock on the bathroom door?'

Original question – 'Were you scared about leaving the hostel?' (leading question)
New question – 'How did you feel about leaving the hostel?'

Original question – 'Do you get on with your neighbours?'
New questions – 'Do you speak to your neighbours?'
'Do your neighbours help you? How?'
'Have you been inside their houses?'

LIVING WITH OTHER PEOPLE

NAME:.............................. TIME OF INTERVIEW:

DATE:............ STARTED:..........ENDED:...........

WHERE YOU LIVED BEFORE

1(a) HOW LONG DID YOU LIVE AT THE HOSTEL?..................................

(b) WHAT WAS IT LIKE LIVING IN THE HOSTEL?

....

....

....

---

2 WHAT HELP DID YOU GET BEFORE LEAVING THE HOSTEL?
(e.g. LEARNING TO GET ON WITH OTHERS IN A SMALL GROUP; LEARNING NEW SKILLS - COOKING, SHOPPING, HANDLING MONEY)

....

....

....

---

3 HOW DID YOU FEEL ABOUT LEAVING THE HOSTEL?

....

....

....

---

4 WHAT'S IT LIKE LIVING AWAY FROM THE HOSTEL?

....

....

....

COMPARED TO WHERE YOU LIVED BEFORE?

VERY BAD	BAD	ALL RIGHT	GOOD	VERY GOOD
☐	☐	☐	☐	☐

PHYSICAL SURROUNDINGS

5 DID YOU COME TO SEE THE HOUSE BEFORE MOVING IN? YES ☐ NO ☐ DON'T KNOW ☐

....

....

....

6 DO YOU LIKE THE WAY THE HOUSE IS DECORATED? YES ☐ NO ☐ DON'T KNOW ☐

DID YOU CHOOSE THE DECORATIONS? YES ☐ NO ☐ DON'T KNOW ☐

(IF NO) WHO CHOSE THE DECORATIONS?

....

....

7 DO YOU LIKE THE FURNITURE? YES ☐ NO ☐ DON'T KNOW ☐

DID YOU CHOOSE YOUR FURNITURE? YES ☐ NO ☐ DON'T KNOW ☐

(IF NO) WHO CHOSE THE FURNITURE?

....

....

8 ARE YOU ALLOWED TO HAVE PETS? YES ☐ NO ☐ DON'T KNOW ☐

....

....

....

COMPARED TO WHERE YOU LIVED BEFORE?

VERY BAD	BAD	ALL RIGHT	GOOD	VERY GOOD
☐	☐	☐	☐	☐

HOUSE RULES/ORGANISATION

9(a) WHO DOES THE COOKING? ....

....

(b) WHO DOES THE HOUSEWORK? ....

....

(c) WHO DOES THE SHOPPING? ....

....

10 HOW DO YOU DECIDE WHO DOES THESE THINGS? ....

....

....

11 DO YOU HAVE ANY HOUSE RULES? (e.g. ABOUT WHEN TO HAVE A BATH; GETTING UP; GOING TO BED; GOING INTO OTHER PEOPLE'S BEDROOMS)

YES ☐ NO ☐ DON'T KNOW ☐

....

....

12 DO YOU EVER SIT DOWN TOGETHER FOR A MEAL? IF YES, HOW OFTEN?

YES ☐ NO ☐ DON'T KNOW ☐

....

....

13 DO YOU HAVE A RESIDENTS' COMMITTEE/ HOUSE MEETING? IF YES, HOW OFTEN?

YES ☐ NO ☐ DON'T KNOW ☐

....

....

COMPARED TO WHERE YOU LIVED BEFORE?

VERY BAD ☐ BAD ☐ ALL RIGHT ☐ GOOD ☐ VERY GOOD ☐

PRIVACY/TRUST (CONFIDENTIALITY)

14 DO THE OTHER PEOPLE IN THE HOUSE KNOCK BEFORE COMING INTO YOUR ROOM?

	YES	NO	DON'T KNOW
DO THE OTHER PEOPLE IN THE HOUSE KNOCK BEFORE COMING INTO YOUR ROOM?	☐	☐	☐
IS THERE A LOCK ON THE BATHROOM DOOR?	☐	☐	☐
CAN YOU BE ON YOUR OWN IN YOUR OWN ROOM IF YOU WANT TO?	☐	☐	☐

....

....

....

---

15 DO YOU TRUST ONE ANOTHER?
(e.g. CAN YOU TRUST PEOPLE NOT TO TAKE MONEY FROM YOUR ROOM?
CAN YOU TELL SECRETS TO THE OTHER RESIDENTS?)

YES	NO	DON'T KNOW
☐	☐	☐

....

....

....

COMPARED TO WHERE YOU LIVED BEFORE?

VERY BAD	BAD	ALL RIGHT	GOOD	VERY GOOD
☐	☐	☐	☐	☐

****

RELATIONSHIPS WITH STAFF/SUPPORT WORKERS

16 WERE THE STAFF IN THE HOUSE CHOSEN BY YOU? YES ☐ NO ☐ DON'T KNOW ☐

....

....

....

17 WHEN ARE STAFF IN THE HOUSE?

....

....

18 HOW OFTEN DO YOU THINK STAFF SHOULD BE HERE?

....

....

19 DO YOU GET ON WITH THE STAFF? YES ☐ NO ☐ DON'T KNOW ☐

....

....

....

20 HOW DO STAFF HELP YOU? (e.g. LEARNING TO COOK, PERSONAL HYGIENE, TALKING ABOUT PROBLEMS)

....

....

....

COMPARED TO WHERE YOU LIVED BEFORE?

VERY BAD ☐ BAD ☐ ALL RIGHT ☐ GOOD ☐ VERY GOOD ☐

RELATIONSHIPS WITH OUTSIDE PROFESSIONALS

21 DO YOU GO TO A GP? YES ☐ NO ☐ DON'T KNOW ☐

....

....

....

---

22 DID YOU CHOOSE YOUR OWN GP? YES ☐ NO ☐ DON'T KNOW ☐

....

....

....

---

23 DO YOU GO TO ANY OTHER PROFESSIONALS TO GET SPECIAL HELP? (e.g. SPEECH THERAPIST, PHYSIOTHERAPIST, OTHER TYPES OF DOCTOR) YES ☐ NO ☐ DON'T KNOW ☐

IF NO, IS THERE ANY SPECIAL HELP YOU WOULD LIKE TO HAVE FROM PEOPLE LIKE THESE?

....

....

....

COMPARED TO WHERE YOU LIVED BEFORE?

VERY BAD	BAD	ALL RIGHT	GOOD	VERY GOOD
☐	☐	☐	☐	☐

****

<u>RELATIONSHIPS WITH RESIDENTS</u>

24 DO YOU GET ON WELL WITH EACH OTHER? (ARGUMENTS,'ATMOSPHERE')

YES ☐ NO ☐ DON'T KNOW ☐

....

....

....

---

25 DID YOU KNOW EACH OTHER BEFORE YOU MOVED INTO THE HOUSE?

YES ☐ NO ☐ DON'T KNOW ☐

IF YES, HOW LONG HAVE YOU KNOWN THEM?

....

....

....

COMPARED TO WHERE YOU LIVED BEFORE?

VERY BAD	BAD	ALL RIGHT	GOOD	VERY GOOD
☐	☐	☐	☐	☐

SOLVING PROBLEMS

26(a) IF YOU HAVE A PROBLEM, WHO DO YOU GO AND SEE?

....

....

(b) CAN YOU CHOOSE WHO YOU WILL TALK TO ABOUT PROBLEMS? (e.g. WOMEN CHOOSING NOT TO TALK ABOUT PERSONAL PROBLEMS WITH MALE MEMBER OF STAFF)

YES ☐ NO ☐ DON'T KNOW ☐

....

....

....

27 DOES YOUR PROBLEM GET SOLVED?

YES ☐ NO ☐ DON'T KNOW ☐

(IF YES, HOW WAS IT SOLVED?)
(IF NO, WHAT WOULD YOU DO NEXT?)

....

....

....

28 WHAT WOULD YOU DO IF SOMETHING VERY SERIOUS HAPPENED? (e.g. SOMEONE WAS BEATEN UP; MONEY WAS STOLEN FROM THE HOUSE)

....

....

....

29 DO YOU HAVE AN OFFICIAL COMPLAINTS PROCEDURE?

YES ☐ NO ☐ DON'T KNOW ☐

....

....

....

COMPARED TO WHERE YOU LIVED BEFORE?

VERY BAD	BAD	ALL RIGHT	GOOD	VERY GOOD
☐	☐	☐	☐	☐

MONEY

30 DO YOU CASH YOUR OWN BENEFIT BOOK? YES ☐ NO ☐ DON'T KNOW ☐

....

....

31 DO YOU PAY YOUR OWN RENT? YES ☐ NO ☐ DON'T KNOW ☐

....

....

32 DO YOU BUY YOUR OWN FOOD YOURSELF? YES ☐ NO ☐ DON'T KNOW ☐

....

....

33 DO YOU HAVE MONEY OF YOUR OWN TO SPEND? YES ☐ NO ☐ DON'T KNOW ☐

....

....

34 CAN YOU GO INTO A SHOP AND BUY A NEWSPAPER OR CAN OF DRINK ON YOUR OWN? YES ☐ NO ☐ DON'T KNOW ☐

....

....

COMPARED TO WHERE YOU LIVED BEFORE?

VERY BAD ☐ BAD ☐ ALL RIGHT ☐ GOOD ☐ VERY GOOD ☐

CLOTHES

35 DO YOU CHOOSE WHAT YOU WEAR? YES ☐ NO ☐ DON'T KNOW ☐

....

....

....

---

36 DO YOU GO OUT AND BUY YOUR OWN CLOTHES? YES ☐ NO ☐ DON'T KNOW ☐

....

....

....

COMPARED TO WHERE YOU LIVED BEFORE?

VERY BAD ☐ BAD ☐ ALL RIGHT ☐ GOOD ☐ VERY GOOD ☐

****

VISITORS

37 CAN PEOPLE VISIT YOU WHENEVER YOU WANT? YES ☐ NO ☐ DON'T KNOW ☐

---

38 WHEN DID YOU LAST HAVE A VISIT FROM - A FAMILY MEMBER?...................

....

- A FRIEND?..........................

....

39 DO YOU MEET OTHER RESIDENTS' VISITORS? YES ☐ NO ☐ DON'T KNOW ☐

....

....

....

COMPARED TO WHERE YOU LIVED BEFORE?

VERY BAD	BAD	ALL RIGHT	GOOD	VERY GOOD
☐	☐	☐	☐	☐

****

NEIGHBOURS/ACQUAINTANCES

40 DO YOU SPEAK TO YOUR NEIGHBOURS? YES ☐ NO ☐ DON'T KNOW ☐

....

....

---

41 DO THEY HELP YOU? YES ☐ NO ☐ DON'T KNOW ☐
IF YES, HOW DO THEY HELP YOU?

....

....

---

42 HAVE YOU BEEN INSIDE THEIR HOUSES? YES ☐ NO ☐ DON'T KNOW ☐

....

....

....

---

43 HOW DO OTHER PEOPLE TREAT YOU?
(e.g. PEOPLE IN THE STREET, AT THE BUS-STOP, SHOP ASSISTANTS)

....

....

....

COMPARED TO WHERE YOU LIVED BEFORE?

VERY BAD	BAD	ALL RIGHT	GOOD	VERY GOOD
☐	☐	☐	☐	☐

****

FRIENDS AND RELATIONSHIPS

44 DO YOU HAVE FRIENDS OTHER THAN PEOPLE WHO LIVE IN THE HOUSE?

YES	NO	DON'T KNOW
☐	☐	☐

....

....

....

---

45 WHERE DID YOU MEET THEM?

....

....

....

---

46 DO YOU HAVE A SPECIAL FRIEND?

YES	NO	DON'T KNOW
☐	☐	☐

....

....

....

---

47 WOULD YOU LIKE TO TELL US MORE ABOUT YOUR FRIENDS?

YES	NO	DON'T KNOW
☐	☐	☐

....

....

....

COMPARED TO BEFORE?

VERY BAD	BAD	ALL RIGHT	GOOD	VERY GOOD
☐	☐	☐	☐	☐

RELIGION/SPIRITUAL/CULTURAL

48 ARE YOU ABLE TO ATTEND A PLACE OF WORSHIP IF YOU WANT TO?

YES ☐ NO ☐ DON'T KNOW ☐

....

....

....

---

49 DO YOU MEET WITH PEOPLE FROM OTHER RELIGIONS?

YES ☐ NO ☐ DON'T KNOW ☐

....

....

....

---

50 DO YOU MEET WITH PEOPLE FROM OTHER CULTURES?

YES ☐ NO ☐ DON'T KNOW ☐

....

....

....

COMPARED TO BEFORE?

VERY BAD ☐ BAD ☐ ALL RIGHT ☐ GOOD ☐ VERY GOOD ☐

****

HOW RESIDENTS FEEL ABOUT THEMSELVES

51 HOW DO YOU FEEL NOW ABOUT DOING THINGS FOR YOURSELF?
(e.g. ABOUT LOOKING AFTER YOURSELF; GOING OUT ON YOUR OWN; MAKING CHOICES)

YES ☐ NO ☐ DON'T KNOW ☐

....

....

....

52 DO YOU FIND IT DIFFICULT TO ASK FOR HELP? YES ☐ NO ☐ DON'T KNOW ☐

....

....

....

---

53 CAN YOU SAY 'NO'? (BEING ASSERTIVE) YES ☐ NO ☐ DON'T KNOW ☐

....

....

....

COMPARED TO WHERE YOU LIVED BEFORE?

VERY BAD ☐ BAD ☐ ALL RIGHT ☐ GOOD ☐ VERY GOOD ☐

****

<u>MAKING YOUR OWN DECISIONS/TAKING RESPONSIBILITY FOR YOUR LIFE</u>

54 CAN YOU GO OUT WHEN YOU WANT TO? YES ☐ NO ☐ DON'T KNOW ☐

....

....

....

---

55 CAN YOU COME BACK WHEN YOU WANT TO? YES ☐ NO ☐ DON'T KNOW ☐

....

....

....

56 CAN YOU HAVE A BATH/CUP OF TEA WHEN YOU WANT TO?

YES ☐ NO ☐ DON'T KNOW ☐

....

....

....

---

57 CAN YOU GO TO THE PUB ON YOUR OWN?

YES ☐ NO ☐ DON'T KNOW ☐

....

....

....

	YES	NO	DON'T KNOW
58(a) DO YOU HAVE YOUR OWN FRONT DOOR KEY?	☐	☐	☐
(b) DO YOU HAVE YOUR OWN BEDROOM DOOR KEY?	☐	☐	☐

....

....

....

---

59 ARE YOU RESPONSIBLE FOR TAKING YOUR OWN MEDICATION?

YES ☐ NO ☐ DON'T KNOW ☐

....

....

....

COMPARED TO WHERE YOU LIVED BEFORE?

VERY BAD	BAD	ALL RIGHT	GOOD	VERY GOOD
☐	☐	☐	☐	☐

****

LEISURE/WEEKENDS/EVENINGS

NAME:..............................

TIME OF INTERVIEW:

DATE:.............

STARTED:..........ENDED:...........

1 WHAT DO YOU DO IN YOUR SPARE TIME?

....

....

....

---

2 WHAT'S YOUR FAVOURITE TV PROGRAMME?

....

....

....

VISITS OUT/GETTING OUT AND ABOUT

	YES	NO	DON'T KNOW
3(a) DO YOU GO OUT ON YOUR OWN?	☐	☐	☐

HOW OFTEN?...

	YES	NO	DON'T KNOW
(b) DO YOU GO OUT WITH OTHER PEOPLE?	☐	☐	☐

HOW OFTEN?...

WHO WITH?..

	YES	NO	DON'T KNOW
4 DO YOU HAVE ANY PROBLEMS TRAVELLING AROUND? (MOBILITY, USING PUBLIC TRANSPORT)	☐	☐	☐

....

....

....

5 WHAT SORT OF PLACES DO YOU ENJOY GOING OUT TO?

....

....

....

---

6 WOULD YOU LIKE TO GO OUT MORE THAN YOU DO NOW?

YES	NO	DON'T KNOW
☐	☐	☐

....

....

....

---

7 ARE THERE ENOUGH THINGS TO DO IN THE LOCAL AREA?

YES	NO	DON'T KNOW
☐	☐	☐

....

....

....

....

COMPARED TO WHERE YOU LIVED BEFORE?

VERY BAD	BAD	ALL RIGHT	GOOD	VERY GOOD
☐	☐	☐	☐	☐

****

<u>HOBBIES</u>

8 WHAT HOBBIES HAVE YOU GOT NOW?

....

....

....

9 ARE THERE ANY OTHER HOBBIES THAT YOU WOULD LIKE TO DO?

YES ☐ NO ☐ DON'T KNOW ☐

....

....

....

---

10 WHO WOULD HELP YOU FIND OUT MORE ABOUT NEW HOBBIES?

....

....

---

11 DO YOU GO TO THE LOCAL LIBRARY?

YES ☐ NO ☐ DON'T KNOW ☐

....

....

---

12 DO YOU READ BOOKS?

YES ☐ NO ☐ DON'T KNOW ☐

....

....

COMPARED TO WHERE YOU LIVED BEFORE?

VERY BAD ☐ BAD ☐ ALL RIGHT ☐ GOOD ☐ VERY GOOD ☐

****

<u>HOLIDAYS</u>

13 WHERE ARE YOU GOING THIS YEAR?..

14 WHO ARE YOU GOING WITH?..

....

15 HAVE YOU BEEN ABROAD?

YES ☐ NO ☐ DON'T KNOW ☐

....

16 WHERE DO YOU USUALLY GO ON HOLIDAY?.......................................

....

17 CAN YOU CHOOSE WHERE YOU WOULD LIKE TO GO?..................................

....

COMPARED TO WHERE YOU LIVED BEFORE?

VERY BAD	BAD	ALL RIGHT	GOOD	VERY GOOD
☐	☐	☐	☐	☐

****

EDUCATION

18 WHAT KIND OF SCHOOL DID YOU GO TO?...

....

19 WHAT WAS LIFE LIKE AT SCHOOL?...

....

	YES	NO	DON'T KNOW
20 DO YOU GO TO A FURTHER EDUCATION COLLEGE?	☐	☐	☐
21 DO YOU GO TO AN ADULT EDUCATION CENTRE?	☐	☐	☐
22 DO YOU GO TO EVENING CLASSES?	☐	☐	☐

IF YES TO ANY OF THESE:

23 WHAT SUBJECTS DO YOU DO?..

....

....

24 WHAT SUBJECTS WOULD YOU LIKE TO DO IN THE FUTURE?

....

....

COMPARED TO WHERE YOU LIVED BEFORE?

VERY BAD	BAD	ALL RIGHT	GOOD	VERY GOOD
☐	☐	☐	☐	☐

DAY CENTRE/WORK QUESTIONNAIRE

NAME:.............................. TIME OF INTERVIEW:

DATE:............. STARTED:............ENDED:.............

DAY CENTRE

1(a) HOW LONG HAVE YOU BEEN COMING TO THIS CENTRE?

....

....

(b) HOW DO YOU FEEL ABOUT COMING HERE?

....

....

....

---

2 WHAT DO YOU LIKE BEST ABOUT IT?

....

....

....

---

3 WHAT DO YOU LIKE LEAST ABOUT IT?

....

....

....

---

4 WHAT TIME DO YOU START? ....AM/PM

WHAT TIME DO YOU FINISH? ....AM/PM

....

....

....

LANGUAGE/'LABELLING'

5 HOW DO STAFF DESCRIBE PEOPLE AT THE CENTRE?

....

....

RELATIONSHIPS WITH STAFF

		YES	NO	DON'T KNOW
6	DO YOU GET ALONG WITH STAFF?	☐	☐	☐
7	DO YOU HAVE A SPECIAL FRIEND AMONG THE STAFF?	☐	☐	☐
8	DO YOU GET ON WITH THE MANAGER?	☐	☐	☐
9	DO YOU ATTEND STAFF MEETINGS?	☐	☐	☐
10	ARE YOU INVOLVED WITH INTERVIEWING FOR NEW STAFF?	☐	☐	☐

....

....

....

RELATIONSHIPS WITH CLIENTS/STUDENTS

		YES	NO	DON'T KNOW
11	DO YOU GET ON WITH THE OTHER CLIENTS/STUDENTS?	☐	☐	☐
12	DO YOU HAVE A SPECIAL FRIEND AMONG THE CLIENTS/STUDENTS?	☐	☐	☐

....

....

13	DO YOU HAVE A CLIENTS'/STUDENTS' COMMITTEE?	☐	☐	☐

IF YES -

14 HOW DO YOU FIND OUT WHAT THE COMMITTEE DOES?

....

....

....

15 HOW DO PEOPLE GET TO BE ON THE COMMITTEE?

....

....

....

---

16 WHAT SORT OF JOBS & ACTIVITIES DO PEOPLE DO AT THE CENTRE?

....

....

....

---

17 CAN YOU CHOOSE WHAT YOU WANT TO DO? YES ☐ NO ☐ DON'T KNOW ☐

....

....

---

18 CAN YOU GO OUT OF THE CENTRE WHEN YOU WANT TO? YES ☐ NO ☐ DON'T KNOW ☐
(WHEN? HOW ORGANISED?)

....

....

19(a) DO YOU GET ANY MONEY FROM THE CENTRE? YES ☐ NO ☐ DON'T KNOW ☐

....

....

(b) HOW DO YOU FEEL ABOUT THIS?

....

....

....

GETTING A JOB

20 WOULD YOU LIKE TO HAVE A JOB OUTSIDE? YES ☐ NO ☐ DON'T KNOW ☐

IF YES, WHAT SORT OF JOB?

....

....

---

21 WHO WOULD HELP YOU GET A JOB?

....

....

....

---

22 DID YOU GO TO ANY OTHER CENTRE BEFORE THIS ONE? YES ☐ NO ☐ DON'T KNOW ☐

IF YES, WHICH ONE DO YOU PREFER?

....

....

....

QUESTIONS TO FAMILY

NAME:............................. TIME OF INTERVIEW:

DATE:...................... STARTED:..............ENDED:

1 HOW DID YOU FEEL WHEN ....
MOVED TO HIS/HER HOME?

....

....

....

---

2 DID YOU GET ANY SPECIAL HELP/SUPPORT BEFORE HE/SHE MOVED INTO THE HOUSE?

YES ☐ NO ☐ DON'T KNOW ☐

IF YES, WHAT KIND OF HELP?
(e.g. HELP FOR MOVING FURNITURE & BELONGINGS;
MONEY; EMOTIONAL SUPPORT)

....

....

....

IF NO, WHAT WOULD HAVE HELPED?

....

....

....

---

3 DO YOU GET ANY SPECIAL HELP/SUPPORT NOW?

YES ☐ NO ☐ DON'T KNOW ☐

IF YES, WHAT KIND?

....

....

....

IF NO, WHAT SORT OF HELP DO YOU FEEL YOU NEED?

....

....

....

4 HAVE YOU NOTICED ANY CHANGES IN........SINCE HE/SHE MOVED TO HIS/HER NEW HOME?

....

....

....

---

5 WHAT CHANGES WOULD YOU LIKE TO SEE IN THE FUTURE FOR HIM/HER?

....

....

....

	YES	NO	DON'T KNOW
6 DO YOU GET ASKED TO GO TO MEETINGS AT HOME WITH..............?	☐	☐	☐
7 DO YOU GET ASKED TO GO TO MEETINGS AT CENTRE WITH............?	☐	☐	☐

....

....

....

---

8 HOW OFTEN DOES................COME TO SEE YOU?

....

....

---

9 HOW OFTEN DO YOU GO TO SEE..................?

....

....

---

10 DO YOU GET ANY HELP WITH MAKING VISITS?
(e.g. TRANSPORT; MONEY FOR FARES)

....

....

....

QUESTIONS TO STAFF IN HOUSES

NAME:............................ TIME OF INTERVIEW:

DATE:.................. STARTED:..........ENDED:............

1 HOW LONG HAVE YOU BEEN HERE?

....

2 WHY DID YOU APPLY FOR THIS JOB?

....

....

....

3 WERE ANY OF THE RESIDENTS INVOLVED IN INTERVIEWING YOU FOR THE JOB?

YES ☐ NO ☐ DON'T KNOW ☐

....

....

....

4 WHAT IS YOUR PAST EXPERIENCE?

....

....

....

5 WHAT ARE THE AIMS OF THIS HOUSE?

....

....

....

6 DO YOU GET ON WITH THE RESIDENTS?

YES ☐ NO ☐ DON'T KNOW ☐

....

....

7 ARE RESIDENTS INVOLVED IN MAKING DECISIONS ABOUT THE HOUSE? YES ☐ NO ☐ DON'T KNOW ☐

....

....

....

---

8 ARE ANY DECISIONS MADE WITHOUT INVOLVING RESIDENTS? YES ☐ NO ☐ DON'T KNOW ☐

....

....

....

---

9 DO YOU HAVE A HOUSE MEETING WITH THE RESIDENTS? YES ☐ NO ☐ DON'T KNOW ☐

....

....

....

---

10 HAVE YOU CHANGED ANYTHING THAT THE RESIDENTS ASKED FOR? YES ☐ NO ☐ DON'T KNOW ☐

....

....

....

---

11 HOW DO YOU INVOLVE PEOPLE IN PLANNING WHAT THEY WANT TO DO? (PERSONAL PLANS/REVIEWS/IPPS)

....

....

....

12(a) HAVE YOU NOTICED ANY CHANGES IN RESIDENTS SINCE YOU HAVE BEEN HERE?

YES ☐ NO ☐ DON'T KNOW ☐

(b) IF YES, WHAT SORT OF CHANGES?

....

....

....

---

13 COULD YOU GIVE SOME EXAMPLES OF CHANGES YOU WOULD LIKE TO SEE IN RESIDENTS IN THE FUTURE?

....

....

....

---

14 WAS THERE ANY LOCAL PROTEST ABOUT SETTING UP THE HOUSE?

YES ☐ NO ☐ DON'T KNOW ☐

....

....

....

---

15 WHAT DO YOU LIKE BEST ABOUT WORKING IN THE HOUSE?

....

....

....

---

16 WHAT DO YOU LIKE LEAST?

....

....

....

QUESTIONS TO CENTRE MANAGERS

NAME:.....................   TIME OF INTERVIEW:

DATE:......................   STARTED:..........ENDED:............

1 HOW LONG HAVE YOU BEEN HERE?

....

....

---

2 WHY DID YOU APPLY FOR THE MANAGER'S JOB?

....

....

....

---

3 WERE ANY PEOPLE WITH LEARNING DIFFICULTIES INVOLVED IN INTERVIEWING YOU FOR THE JOB?

YES	NO	DON'T KNOW
☐	☐	☐

....

....

....

---

4 WHAT IS YOUR PAST EXPERIENCE?

....

....

....

---

5 WHAT ARE THE AIMS OF THE CENTRE?

....

....

....

6 DO YOU CONSULT WITH THE CLIENTS ABOUT THE AIMS OF THE CENTRE?

YES ☐ NO ☐ DON'T KNOW ☐

....

....

....

---

7 HAVE YOU CHANGED ANYTHING SINCE YOU HAVE BEEN HERE?

YES ☐ NO ☐ DON'T KNOW ☐

....

....

....

---

8 HAVE YOU CHANGED ANYTHING THAT THE STUDENTS ASKED FOR?

YES ☐ NO ☐ DON'T KNOW ☐

....

....

....

---

9 DO YOU GET ON WITH STUDENTS/CLIENTS

....

....

....

---

10 DO YOU GET ON WITH THE STAFF?

....

....

....

11 DO STUDENTS/CLIENTS ATTEND STAFF MEETINGS?

YES ☐ NO ☐ DON'T KNOW ☐

....

....

....

---

12 HOW DO YOU INVOLVE PEOPLE IN PLANNING WHAT THEY WANT TO DO? (PERSONAL PLANS/REVIEWS/IPPS)

....

....

....

---

13 HOW MANY PEOPLE FROM THE CENTRE HAVE GOT AN ORDINARY JOB WITHIN:

THE LAST SIX MONTHS: THE LAST YEAR:

....

....

....

---

14 DO YOU HAVE PEOPLE FROM MINORITY GROUPS AT THE CENTRE?

....

....

....

---

15 WHAT THINGS WOULD YOU LIKE TO SEE HAPPEN AT THE CENTRE IN THE FUTURE?

....

....

....

****

QUESTIONS TO SENIOR MANAGERS

NAME:................................ TIME OF INTERVIEW:

DATE:................................ STARTED:..........ENDED:...........

1 HOW LONG HAVE YOU BEEN HERE?

....

....

....

---

2 WHY DID YOU APPLY FOR THIS JOB?

....

....

....

---

3 WERE ANY PEOPLE WITH LEARNING DIFFICULTIES INVOLVED IN INTERVIEWING FOR THE JOB?

YES ☐ NO ☐ DON'T KNOW ☐

....

....

---

4 WHAT IS YOUR PAST EXPERIENCE?

....

....

....

---

5 WHAT IS YOUR ROLE & YOUR RESPONSIBILITY IN THIS POST?

....

....

....

6 DO YOU CONSULT WITH THE RESIDENTS ABOUT WHAT THEY WANT FROM THE SERVICE?

YES ☐ NO ☐ DON'T KNOW DAF JAH

IF YES, HOW?

....

....

....

7 HAVE YOU CHANGED ANYTHING SINCE YOU HAVE BEEN HERE?

YES ☐ NO ☐ DON'T KNOW ☐

....

....

---

8 HAVE YOU CHANGED ANYTHING THAT THE RESIDENTS ASKED FOR?

YES ☐ NO ☐ DON'T KNOW ☐

....

....

....

9(a) DO YOU GET ON WITH STUDENTS/CLIENTS/ RESIDENTS?

YES ☐ NO ☐ DON'T KNOW ☐

....

....

....

(b) HOW DO YOU DESCRIBE PEOPLE IN THE HOUSES?

....

....

....

10(a) DO YOU GET ON WITH THE STAFF? YES ☐ NO ☐ DON'T KNOW ☐

....

....

....

(b) HOW DO YOU SUPPORT STAFF IN WHAT THEY DO?

....

....

....

---

11 DO STUDENTS/CLIENTS ATTEND STAFF MEETINGS? YES ☐ NO ☐ DON'T KNOW ☐

....

....

....

---

12 HOW DO YOU INVOLVE PEOPLE IN PLANNING WHAT THEY WANT TO DO? (PERSONAL PLANS/REVIEWS/IPPS)

....

....

....

---

13 HOW DO YOU HELP CLIENTS HANDLE THEIR OWN MONEY?

....

....

14 CAN RESIDENTS MAKE A COMPLAINT TO YOU?

....

....

---

15 HOW MANY PEOPLE HAVE GOT AN ORDINARY JOB WITHIN:

THE LAST SIX MONTHS:........... THE LAST YEAR:.............

....

....

....

16(a) HOW MANY PEOPLE FROM MINORITY GROUPS ARE EMPLOYED BY YOUR SERVICE?

....

(b) HOW MANY CLIENTS COME FROM AN ETHNIC MINORITY?

....

---

17 HOW WERE THE STAFF IN THE HOUSES CHOSEN?

....

....

---

18 HOW MANY SPEECH THERAPISTS HAVE YOU GOT?

....

---

19 WHAT THINGS WOULD YOU LIKE TO SEE HAPPEN IN THE FUTURE?

....

....

....

****

13 Other 'tools' we used

The sad-to-happy faces

An enlarged version of this picture of five faces was mounted on card and used to help residents answer the questions which compared their lives now to what they were like before.

Resident 'profile'

The evaluation team were given information about each resident's weekly activities before the evaluation began. This information was made up into a chart as the sample below shows.

	(Name)		(Name)		(Name)	
	DAY	EVE.	DAY	EVE.	DAY	EVE.
MON.	Day Centre (occ. work experience Express Dairy)	Cookery Class	6.15am 5.30pm Cleaner for at (not happy about visiting work)	In House	Day Centre	Cooks meal; cleans birds; Tapes or TV
TUES	"	In house	"	In house	"	"
WED.	"	In house	"	In house	"	"
THU.	"	Gateway Club	"	In house	"	"
FRI.	"	In house	"	In house	"	"
SAT.	Sainsburys	Housework	Sainsburys	Housework	Sainsburys	Housework
SUN.	In house (visits sister once month)	In house	In house (very occasionally visits his family)	In house	In house (occasionally sees brother)	In house

Notes prepared by the evaluation team before visiting the homes

What we need to talk to the residents about at the first meeting

1. DO THEY KNOW THE MEANING OF THE WORD EVALUATION? (e.g. improving services; improving where you live; making people's lives better.)

2. WE ARE NOT EVALUATING THEM, WE ARE EVALUATING THE SERVICE.
   WE ARE TRYING TO HELP STAFF TO HELP PEOPLE WITH LEARNING DIFFICULTIES HAVE A BETTER LIFE.
   BY AGREEING TO TAKE PART, THEY WILL BE HELPING OTHER PEOPLE WITH LEARNING DIFFICULTIES TO HELP THEMSELVES.

3. ARE THERE ANY PARTICULAR TOPICS THEY WOULD LIKE TO TALK TO US ABOUT?

4. ARE THERE ANY TOPICS THEY WANT US TO KEEP STRICTLY CONFIDENTIAL?

5. CAN WE TALK TO THEIR PARENTS/FRIENDS/RELATIVES?

6. WHO IS THEIR KEY WORKER/MAIN SUPPORT PERSON?

Aims for the first meeting – Friday, 16th and Saturday, 17th March

1. START TO GET TO KNOW THE PEOPLE IN THE HOUSES.

2. MAKE SURE THEY UNDERSTAND WHAT WE ARE DOING.

3. TELL THEM HOW WE PLAN TO DO THE EVALUATION.

4. WORK OUT A TIMETABLE FOR THE NEXT TWO WEEKS.

PART IV

OTHER USEFUL INFORMATION

Appendices
References
Further reading
Addresses

Appendices

Appendix A: Experiences of working to develop self-advocacy

Simon Gardner

I first got involved with Wandsworth Disability Association (WDA) in July 1988 when they were planning a conference on education and integration for children and adults with learning difficulties. My ex-boss from the Community Aide Programme where I work was asked if she knew of anyone willing to help and she suggested me.

I helped with the general 'nitty gritty' of organising the conference – looked into the accessibility of the building; organised the buffet; etc.

Now I am a member of the WDA Joint Education sub-committee (Integration Alliance) which was set up soon after the conference. It is a London-wide body.

I agreed to be a member of this sub-committee because I am particularly interested in integration of children and adults with learning difficulties in schools; access for people in wheelchairs; facilities for teachers who are disabled.

I went to a special school for people who are partially sighted. I had a good teacher in the beginning, from age of 5 to 11. After that, for about two or three years, I had every teacher in the school! I got behind with my work and had a horrible time until the last two years when a special class was set up. I left at age 15/16.

I went to a Rudolph Steiner School. I hated it because there was no TV, no radio, nothing. I was there about a month and left. I rang up my uncle and he came and picked me up.

I went to a school in Redhill for Further Education and Training. The first month was fine but after two months the education cuts came in so I had to leave because the Borough of Merton wouldn't pay any more money. I was back to square one.

Then I went to an ATC in Mitcham. I hated that and left after a year or so. I didn't like being pushed around by staff younger than myself.

How self-advocacy has helped me

Being involved in self-advocacy gave me an interest. Before, I only had myself and four walls. I have been involved since the setting up of People First, although I took two years off to sort out where I was going.

I like going out and speaking. I find it easier to speak to a large audience than to one or two people. To stand in front of an audience gives me a buzz. In the early years I went to Sheffield and to Wolverhampton. I recently went to a very good conference in Cheshire. I've been going around with People First and John Hersov, and doing disability awareness training. I want to pass on my experience of what has happened to me and going through the system of education and fighting the system and proving people (practitioners, doctors, and so on) wrong.

They said I'd never be independent; that I would always have to be helped all the time. I had that round my neck and tried to take it away and keep on fighting for myself and other people less fortunate than myself.

I belong to Westminster People First. We are doing a course on assertiveness training. This has been very successful. It will help us be more assertive as a group and able to run the group better.

I want to start a People First group in Wandsworth. I have been in touch with one of the Wandsworth group homes and asked for names and addresses to get the group going, and have had a meeting at the WDA about getting an advisor.

I was also involved in a group at the WDA studying assertiveness in trying to get employment but it hasn't met for some time. There were five or six people in the group – all with disabilities but not learning difficulties.

Recently I took part in a conference organised by Wandsworth Social Services about community care. We discussed attitudes – with social workers, boroughs and local authorities as a whole, and health managers – and discrimination against people with learning difficulties coming out of long-stay hospitals. Wandsworth Authority is paying Banstead Hospital so much a year to keep people in there. When they come back out their parents are dead, but because their parents lived in Wandsworth, the Borough of Wandsworth is responsible for them. They can't leave the borough as easily as some people. If they moved to Scotland, the Authority in Wandsworth would still be responsible for them.

The conference had a section for People First. I told them about King's Fund and People First and how it started.

A lot of staff in the morning session used words like 'mental handicap', 'mentally impaired', 'dumb', 'imbecile' and so on. In the afternoon I told them not to use those words. I don't want to be ageist, but in my experience, social workers and practitioners who have been in the job 25 years, are not open to new ideas. They still stick to the same labels and the same methods as when they started. I tried to be as tactful as I could!

In my group there were three social workers, one member of staff from an ATC, a member of staff from a Wandsworth group home. They still used the words 'mental handicap'. In the end I said 'Shut up: I am going to tell you what I have been through because of rules and regulations'. They were gob smacked! They still treated me as a second-class citizen. 'I am not a second class citizen. I pay my taxes and pay my rates'. The way they talked down to me. I said 'Don't talk down to me. Treat me as an equal. All that's wrong is I am partially sighted, I have coordination problems, and dyslexia. I am not stupid. I know what you are talking about.'

I couldn't have said that four or five years ago.

Appendix B: Huddersfield People First

Joyce Kershaw

How it all started

Huddersfield SEC used to have a Centre committee meeting on Fridays. One day, the manager brought them a leaflet about CMH and self-advocacy: he thought they would be interested in it. This led to a meeting with Alan le Broc, who became one of their advisors.

They decided to form a group and Joyce and a friend went round talking to people about it and asking if they were interested in joining, and also finding out more about self-advocacy. They spent several months doing this. The first meeting of the group was on 19 August 1986.

Getting support

Joyce contacted people in social services and asked for help. They said that if the group did some fund-raising of their own, they would help with money too. So the group raised money through sponsored events, jumble sales, etc. Social Services have given them a grant every year since. In 1988 it was £700 – bigger than usual, to help with paying fees for people to attend the People First International Conference. This year it is £400 – £100 to the group and £300 to pay for a part-time advisor. The advisor helps them 4 hours a week – gets paid £32 a month. Joyce looks after the money and pays the advisor.

Becoming more independent

They wanted to meet away from the centre. The local co-op runs a community centre, which seemed a good place. It wasn't all 'plain sailing' deciding to have meetings there, though. They had to decide whether they wanted to become a member of the co-op. But if they had done this, they would have had to use the co-op name in front of People First. They didn't want to do this because they wanted to be independent. Also they would have had to pay their funds into the co-op's bank account; if the group broke up their remaining funds would go to the co-op.

They didn't want this: they said that if they thought they were running down, they would give their money away bit by bit to other People First groups!

The co-op also didn't want any other organisation's name to be associated with the group, e.g. they didn't want them to publicise the names of anyone else who might give the group money. The group didn't like this either – they wanted to be able to thank other people who might help them.

So they decided to be independent of the co-op and now meet there without charge – and without any restrictions being put on what they do.

Getting known locally

Their local paper is good at giving them publicity. Joyce negotiates with staff who work there. She persuaded them to change the words they use to describe people: they now use the term 'people with learning difficulties'. On one occasion they printed a photograph with 'mentally handicapped' in the caption. Joyce wrote a letter complaining – received an apology from the paper – and the mistake has never happened again.

The local mayor has been an enthusiastic supporter of each of their three birthday parties.

Getting rid of labels

Joyce always speaks up when people use the term 'mentally handicapped'. Self-advocacy has helped her to be able to do that. 'It's no good just saying it once and thinking they will remember. You have to keep on until you get it through to them.'

Getting people to talk in 'plain English'

Joyce is keen on getting people to talk in words everyone can understand. If they use long words she always asks them to talk in simpler words. For example: she saw the word 'participation' – asked their advisor what it meant. The advisor said: 'joining in'. Joyce said: 'Well, why can't they *say* that!'

Helping to change things within social services

Joyce is now a member of the social services Equal Opportunities sub-committee. When she first began to go to the meetings they would send her 'a right pile of thick papers!' which she couldn't understand. Now they send her a simpler version, concentrating on those items which she is particularly interested in. They also do braille versions of the papers for people who are blind.

How self-advocacy has helped group members

When the group first started people used to be very timid and unsure of themselves – they used to get upset and run to the staff for help. Now the group sorts out its own troubles. People have learnt such a lot, their friends and family can hardly believe how they have changed – grown more independent and able to do so much more for themselves.

One of the first things the group campaigned for was housing – the chance to live a more independent life. Senior people from social services came to the group to listen to what they wanted. Now some have got their own flats or share a house or flat with a friend. More people have got jobs now too.

How the group has helped other people with learning difficulties

Members of the group go out to various places to speak to people about self-advocacy and starting a group. They mostly go on these visits on their own – 'if we want to be independent, then we have to show that we can do it on our own'. Some of the places they have been to are Nottingham, Leeds, London and Birmingham.

They have produced a folder to help people who want to become involved in self-advocacy. It costs £2.00 inclusive of postage.

The future

Huddersfield People First is now getting together with other self-advocates from Yorkshire and are arranging joint meetings with people from Lancashire.

References

1. Whittaker, A. (ed.) *Supporting Self-Advocacy*. London, King's Fund Centre, 1991.
2. Connelly, N. *Raising Voices* Social Services departments and people with disabilities – Chapter 3. London, Policy Studies Institute, 1990.
3. Cragg, R., and Harrison, J. *Living in a Supervised Home (Staffed or Unstaffed). A Questionnaire on Quality of Life*. Birmingham, Campaign for People with a Mental Handicap, 1986.
4. Conroy, J.W., and Bradley, V.J. *The Penhurst Longitudinal Study: A Report of Five Years Research and Analysis*. Philadelphia, Temple University Developmental Disabilities Centre, 1985.
5. O'Brien, J. *A guide to personal futures planning*. In Bellamy, G.T. and Wilcox, B. (eds) *A comprehensive guide to the activities catalog: an alternative curriculum for youth and adults with severe disabilities*. Baltimore, Maryland, Paul JH. Brookes, 1986.
6. Independent Development Council for People with Mental Handicap. *Pursuing Quality – How good are your local services for people with mental handicap?* London, King's Fund Centre, 1986.
7. Norfolk Social Services Department. *Tell us what it's really like*. The experience of 37 volunteers recruited by Age Concern, Norfolk. Norfolk Social Services Department, 1989.
8. PSSRU. *Care in the Community: The First Steps*. Ed. J. Renshaw et al., University of Kent, 1988.
9. Howie, D., Cuming, J. and Raynes, N. *Development of tools to facilitate participation by moderately retarded persons in residental evaluation procedures*. British Journal of Mental Subnormality, 30, 2, 59, 92–8, 1984.
10. Willcocks, D. *The 'ideal home' visual game: a method of consumer research in old people's homes*, Research, Policy and Planning, 2, 1, 13–18, 1984.

Further reading

The following list is aimed at directing readers to a few key references relevant to this subject. None of the references is a very long read! Most of them contain useful reference lists for further reading.

Beresford P, Croft S. *Citizen Involvement: A Practical Guide For Change*. Macmillan (forthcoming).

Booth T, Simons K, Booth W. *Outward Bound. Re-location and community care for people with learning difficulties*. Open University Press, 1990.

Connolly N. *Raising Voices: Social Services departments and people with disabilities*. Policy Studies Institute, 1990.

Whittaker A. *Involving People With Learning Difficulties In Meetings*. In *Power To The People*. ed Liz Winn. King's Fund Centre, 1990.

Winn L, Quick A. *User friendly services: Guidelines for managers for community health services*. King's Fund Centre, 1989.

Addresses

Charities Evaluation Services, Forbes House, 9 Artillery Lane, London E1 7LP. Tel: 071–377 2939.

Community Living Development Team, The King's Fund Centre, 126 Albert Street, London, NW1 7NF. Tel: 071–267 6111.

People First, People First Office, Oxford House, London E2 6HG. Tel: 071–739 3890.